# THIRD WORLD DEVELOPMENT EXPERIENCE

# THIRD WORLD DEVELOPMENT EXPERIENCE

## —TANZANIA

**S. Chandrasekhar**

**1990**

**DAYA PUBLISHING HOUSE**

DELHI - 110006

ISBN 81-7035-092-1



Published by: Anil Mittal for Daya Publishing House at 1302, Vaid Wara, Nai Sarak, Delhi-110006. Phone: 260116.
Laser Typeset by Computer Codes, Delhi-110009.
Printed at D.K. Fine Art Press, Delhi-110052.

**PRINTED IN INDIA**

## *DEDICATION*

This work is dedicated to Professor B. Sarveswara Rao, M.A., Ph.D. (Cantab), Professor Emeritus, in partial fulfilment of a deep debt of gratitude.

## DEDICATION

This work is dedicated to Professor B. Sarveswara Rao, M.A., [illegible] (Cantab), Professor Emeritus, in partial fulfilment of a deep debt of gratitude.

# Preface

That the third world development processes have to undergo pertinent changes if their goals have to be meaningful from the point of the present and future generations needs no reiteration, looked at from the contemporaneous experience of various economies, particularly those economies which have been experiencing persistently precarious levels and patterns of growth in the African continent. And this has been happening in spite of the available better development experience elsewhere. What the large African economies generally require are, given the availability of crucial resources, (*a*) greater interaction with the other developing societies, (*b*) greater participation of the advanced societies and the international agencies in the development processes, so as to associate the required technology and capital to them, (*c*) revise the very ideology of political and economic development with a more realistic outlook that befits the local framework, local resources, and the incentives of the people, and finally (*d*) evolve a public policy consistent with the requirement of tax policy, trade policy and development policy and help minimise the burden of public activity on the fisc, as well as on the public itself. This requires that the public economy shall associate itself with activities consistent with sound finance and productivity. The experience of Tanzania has been examined in order to highlight some of the problems under the present system of organization of the economy, briefly though.

S. CHANDRASEKHAR

# Contents

# List of Tables

# Introduction

Tanzania is a large territory, having a land area of about 3.6 lakh square miles—roughly the same size as Nigeria, almost as the whole of Pakistan or as Venezuela, and nearly 30 per cent larger than Texas. A considerable part of population and economic activity is concentrated in various areas around the periphery because much of the centre of the territory is arid bush country. The main populated areas are linked with roads and railways, highly inadequate though, and distances and dispersion are themselves obstacles to development, making transport a costly proposition, which complicates all administration. The most important ethnic groups of Tanzania are Sukuma, Nyanwazi, Ha, Makonda, and Gogo, generally speak the Swahiti dialect and the English language. Sisal, Coffee, Cotton, Pyrethrum, Cloves, and Sugar have been the most important crops, which are also the chief export items.

Tanzania consists of the mainland Tanganyika and the small offshore island territory of Zanzibar. These territories were united in 1964. More than 120 ethnic groups live in Tanzania and there are small European, Asian and Arab minorities. Tanzania has a farming economy, mostly subsistence, but cash crops form the bulk of the exports. A one-party state, Tanzania has implemented a self-help policy called Uzamaa, whereby people are brought together to work in cooperative villages. Tanzania was a German colony from the 1880s to 1918, when Britain took over. Tanganyika became independent in 1961 and Zanzibar in 1963. Two of the country's main problems are unreliable rainfall in the interior and a poorly developed communication system, which has been improved by the completion of the Tanzania—Zambia railway.

The development problems of Tanzania are extremely heterogeneous, differing widely from one area of another. The case of the relatively prosperous Wachagga, with their bananas and coffee grown at the slopes of Mount Kilimanjaro, in no way resembles that of their neighbours the Masai, the nomadic cattle herders of the arid plains. The problems of Wasukuma, peasant cotton growers to the south of lake victoria, are very different from those of the Wagogo in the centre of the territory, a people under the constant threat of famine caused by failure of rains. Some 120 tribal groupings exist in Tanzania with different customs and habits, adapted to the widely varying conditions in which they live. It is therefore difficult and often misleading to generalize about a territory so large and so diversified.

The natural increase of the African population is believed to be fairly slow, and the death rates are high, while the birth rates are comparatively low. The overall density of population of Tanzania, has also been quite low, and therefore, it may be said that it has no problem of population pressure analogous to that of many Asian Countries. Less than 10 per cent of the land is cultivated, though a considerably larger proportion is grazed. However, population density and land use have to be seen in relation to the low productive potential of much of the land. In some parts, particularly in the highland areas, there has been some land hunger. Tribal boundaries and personal attachment to the native environment hinder movements of population, and so tend to freeze the present uneven distribution and to prevent people from moving from unproductive or overcrowded areas to more favoured places.

In Tanzania, peasant cultivators and nomadic and semi-nomadic cattle keepers form by far the largest part of the population. Trade and some aspects of small scale manufacturing has largely been in the hands of the Indians, Pakistanis, Goans, and Arabs, while a sizeable proportion of them have also been associated with administration, banking and tourism.

Agricultural and livestock development seems to be the persistent preoccupation of the economy, as these products together contribute the most major share of the Gross Domestic Product and the export earnings as well. The next two activities are exploitation of minerals and industrial manufacturers which are relatively insignificant, though. These activities have been quite slow in their progress for various reasons, and in particular due to the slower pace of growth of internal markets.

For a long time, the large estates owned and managed by Europeans or Indians were the major producers of export crops, producing virtually all the sisal and tea, the greater part of tobacco, wheat, pyrethrum and seed beans and peas, and some of the coffee. The contribution of European estate farming to the economy of Tanzania was significant in terms of the participation of the people in the modern production processes, in spite of the fact that, the estates occupied only about one per cent of the total agricultural land. At the same time, the peasant producers have been accounting for about half of exports of crops and about a little more than half of all the marketed crops, while the livestock have been almost entirely African owned.

The physical environment of Tanzania seems to be least conducive for the advancement of agricultural operations. The reasons are as follows :

(*a*) rainfall is low in annual total amount over much of the country;

(*b*) rainfall is everywhere seasonal, thus limiting the production of annual crops to only part of the year. In some areas, where there are two good rainy seasons a year, or one long rainy season, perennial crops can be grown and good yields of annuals are possible. Over much of the country, however, there is only a short rainy season followed by a long, severe dry season, with the result that perennial crops cannot be grown, annual crops must be restricted to quick maturing, drought resistant species, and yields are low. In these areas pasturage for stock is very meagre during the dry season;

(*c*) much of the rainfall occurs in storms of high intensity, during which a large part of the precipitation, runs off the soil surface, and is thus lost to the crops. This is especially important in areas where there is a low total rainfall in a short wet season;

(*d*) rainfall over most of the country is unreliable, varying greatly in total amount from year to year and in its distribution between months within the rainy season. Thus, over much of the country the low total amount and seasonal character of the rainfall, result in many rivers and streams drying out completely during the dry search, which means that a sizeable part of the territory is

> virtually uninhabitable unless artificial water supplies can be provided during the dry season. Fortunately, however, the country is endowed with extensive areas of fertile volcanic soils in parts of highlands in the Northern, Southern, and Southern highlands areas, and alluvial soils in the larger river valleys, and if their use is organized in conjunction with favourable irrigation possibilities, the soils may become a scarce asset which should be developed efficiently and protected against deterioration.

The state of the economy in the 1950s, 1960s, and until about the year 1975, witnessed prosperity based on steadily rising exports, and commerce and industry advancing slowly and steadily, in spite of the fact that it remained a low productivity economy, at the lower end of the international income scale. Production of cash crops was generally looked on as an activity taking second place to production of food for the family.

The problems of the economy seem to have started in the beginning of the 1970s itself with the growing importance of socialist transformation. The socialist strategy was adopted in the year 1967 with the Arusha Declaration. This involves the achievement of three important objectives. The first is the achievement of equality, both materially and in terms of status, and this entails the satisfaction of basic needs and equal participation of all people in the socio economic processes. The second is the eradication of poverty, illiteracy and ill health and general raising of the standard of living of the citizens of Tanzania. This entails the commitment of efforts and resources towards growth of the economy. The third is the attainment of self-reliance in the development process with the help of domestic resources to the extent possible. It entails the achievement of self-sustained independent economy in the long run, whose production and consumption structures are integrated with domestic resource base. But "achievement of equity at the early stage of development in the absence of substantial injection of substantial investible resources from outside a given economy would definitely tend to lower rates of growth". "Equity is attainable at this level only if lower levels of growth are acceptable. The trade off definitely exists since equity tends to increase the consumption proportion and investment share in non-surplus generating sectors such as social services". Secondly, "when an economy chooses to go along the path of self-reliance, it chooses also to grow at a rate compatible with its own resource base and efforts". The growth path generates resource gaps, and therefore, as resources are diverted into social amenities and subsidizing of basic needs, the problem further accentuates, leaving much less for increasing productive capacity, thus adding to the first issue. Thus, the economy having grown somewhat faster upto about the mid 1970s in terms of fixed capital formation, increased investment in the directly productive sectors, increased investment in social services, and thereafter started feeling the crunch for resources at the end of the 1970s, particularly consequent to the Kagera war expenditure in 1978. The resource constraint, the increasing trade gap, growing external debt, increasing trade gap, falling investment in agriculture and decreased investment in infrastructure, have affected the economy in the subsequent years, with rapid inflation taking its role, all attributed to "overzealousness to effect structural change". Also, "Tanzania followed the path of overtaxing the agricultural sector and heavily emphasizing the industrial sector". "The agricultural sector was starved of investment despite being the main contributor to GNP and the main generator of foreign exchange".

Agricultural production registered a rapid decline after the mid 1970s, and the trend has been even more negative in the case of the export crops, owing to the basic causes such as inadequate mechanization, outdated methods of farming, inadequate investments, lack of suitable irrigation, large scale illiteracy on the part of the farmer, lack of suitable seeds, and the intervention of the government in all activities including agriculture in some form of public enterprise which are known as the parastatals, and the ultimate cause, *i.e.*, lack of suitable incentives to participate in the production processes, particularly with the ending of estate farming.

As early as in the year 1961, the economic Mission organized by the International Bank for Reconstruction and Development pointed out that "estate agriculture under non-African management presents very much less extensive problems for public policy than does African agriculture", and that "estate agriculture on alienated land makes a valuable contribution to the economy of the territory, and that policies hostile to the continuance of estate agriculture would be shortsighted". Although the estates were relatively small in total, the value of their product per acre was several times that of

African farming. Thus the estates accounted for around 45 per cent of the value of agricultural exports and some 35 per cent of the value of the total marketed agricultural product. The activity of the estates in the past made an important contribution to the government revenue of Tanzania, the sisal estates in particular among the main income tax payers of the economy. They also had a certain value in demonstrating to Africans relatively advanced methods of production.

The dismal performance of agriculture in particular has generally been attributed to the too many policies which were formulated. "Policies enunciated in the peasant agricultural area have been numerous, some of a general nature, others more specific". One of them is socialism and rural development with its emphasis on the development of Ujamaa villages. The Iringa Resolution on 'politics is agriculture' emphasized the need to modernize agricultural operations. The Moshi Resolution on irrigation urged the population to make use of the "very many water resources" instead of depending upon rain water which has not been dependable. "There is therefore no dearth of policies, if anything there have been too many of them, and sometimes too frequent. When one looks at the performance of these aspects, a gloomy picture emerges. Over a number of years the performance level has been bad. Production in most of the traditional export crops has either declined or stagnated generally; even the production of food crops has not been encouraging. There is an observable inverse proportion trend between the number of policies enunciated and the actual crop output".

The Ujamaa policy had several objectives, some social, some political and some economic. The economic rationale, according to Julius Nyerere is the person "who is working for himself and for his own benefit will not suffer from exploitation in his employment". But he will not make much progress. "It is not long before an individual working alone reaches the limits of his powers; only by working together can men overcome that limitation. The truth is that when men want to make progress they have no alternative but to combine their efforts". According to Nyerere, progress can be made in three stages. "The first may be to persuade people to move their houses into a single village, if possible near water, and to plant their next year's food crops within easy reach of the areas where their houses will be. For another step is to persuade a group of people—perhaps numbers of a ten house cell—to start a small communal plot sharing the proceeds at harvest time according to the work they could have done. Once these steps have been effected, the final stage would come when the people have confidence in a community farm; so that they are willing to invest all their efforts in it simply keeping gardens around their own houses. Then the socialist village would be established and other productive community activities can get under way".

By 1972, several villages had been established with different populations and different shades, but all designated Ujamaa villages. An assessment of the implementation of the policy particularly with regard to the agriculture development aspects of it, indicates vividly that it was almost a flop. "In only very few cases did peasants go beyond the second stage, stipulated in the policy", mainly due to the negative response of the peasants, and ineffective communication between the policy makers, policy implementing officers, and the farmers. "It is very true that through Ujamaa villages the government managed to provide the population with essential social amenities to the extent that was possible, but all this investment has not instilled in the population the necessary spirit to increase agriculture productivity, let alone socialist agricultural development".

John Due and Jean Due, in a working paper of 1983 on East African economies pointed out that the growth experience of the entire region has been very disappointing. "Agricultural production per capita has declined steadily, and in the most recent years, total industrial output has fallen. One consequence has been the seriously increasing foreign debt burden, aggravated by heavy borrowing in the past decade for development projects, many of which have not been as successful as hoped. The causes of the disappointing performance are explored. Defective government policies, particularly the paying of low prices to farmers for agricultural produce, overvalued exchange rates, and misdirected industrial development programmes have played a major role, as has the world recession". In Tanzania, "high export taxes and inefficient marketing boards reduced the domestic terms of trade for export crops by one third in the 1970s; in addition, inputs were diverted from export crops to Ujamaa villages agriculture from the mid 1970s onwards. It is not surprising, therefore, that the volume of exports fell materially". The other problems documented are (*a*) the panterritorial pricing of basic crops resulting in serious misallocation of resources, (*b*) the marketing of the domestic and export markets being placed solely in the hands of government monopolies and marketing boards, (*c*) fear of expatriate domination in marketing organizations, (*d*) agricultural inputs such as seeds, fertilizers and pesticides being controlled by government organizations, and (*e*) spurious foreign exchange rates which were let at such a level as to overvalue the currency. Syeeda Bano pointed out that "the official exchange rate has been kept artificially very high as manifesticed in the accelerated rate of inflation and by about a six-fold parallel market rate, coexistence of this dual exchange rates tends to create distortions in the markets and inefficiencies due to resource shifts from productive to speculative activities. Furthermore, evidence also shows that Tanzania's imports tend to grow faster than the rate of growth of national income and productivity. Specific measures are urgently needed to reverse this trend specially when the trade partners of this country are primarily western world. Reverse flow of resources from an LDC to a developed country like the UK takes place due to outflow of domestic income which in its turn exacerbate the balance of payments problem".

The other important and distressing features have been in terms of the (*a*) exodus of commercial farmers, (*b*) the disappointing performance of the manufacturing sector which has very little comparative advantage, and absorbs a very large proportion of the total available foreign exchange, while very little value was added by this sector (*c*) the industry has become artificially capital intensive, wages have been artificially high, and the scope for increasing employment opportunities has fallen, (*d*) and the most important bottleneck relates to the inadequate infrastructure in terms of rural roads, urban roads, railways and other communication media what with the high petroleum prices; and (*e*) finally, the dependence of the government on a relatively high percentage of tax revenue to GDP with an unacceptable ratio of direct and indirect taxes, and substantial dificits in the current budgets, looked at from the point of the level of development the country has registered. John Due and Jean Due point out that "the indent is that the recurrent budget should provide a surplus and thus savings for financing of development projects; instead, taxes do not cover recurrent costs. Thus not only is potential capital formation lessened, but domestic inflation results. The political pressures for expenditures and demands of government employees for wage increases are so great that, despite the good performance of the tax structures, the deficits have not been avoided".

In general, on the basis of the economic performance, the outlook for future seems to be quite discouraging. The worldwide economic dynamics, the disadvantages of a southern developing society particularly one of the African community, the high energy costs, the natural calamities, and the inconsistent domestic policies have all had serious deterring effects all along. But breaking away from the existing policies involves its own costs, displeasure, time frame, and consequent inconveniences. The foreign debt situation also will continue to hang over the economy "like a dark cloud—but the foreign creditors have little choice but to extend interest and repayment periods, and to accept some cancellation of debt.

# 1

# Financing Development in Tanzania —The Inflation Context

## Introduction

Tanzania, which is one of the most backward economies of the world, has been showing perpetual signs of poverty and underdevelopment. Its problems seem to have accelerated since about the mid 1970s, in terms of inflation, scarcities, shortages, and overall instability.[1] Deficit financing caused by mounting public expenditures, growing taxation, excess money supply, decline in production, and rampant speculation seem to have paralysed the economy in all its dimensions. With the exit of the foreign capital and private enterprise after Tanzania achieved its Independence in the mid sixties, the public sector emerged as an inevitable force for achieving the goals of development.[2] The economic and social philosophy of Tanzania are generally based upon socialism and equality with tolerance towards private sector, and economic openness necessitated by international dependence of kinds. This paper highlights some aspects of the development process with suitable reference to development finance, and is to be considered by no means exhaustive or comprehensive in the approach.

In Tanzania, the most important taxes are, the personal income tax, the corporation income tax, customs and excise duty, and the sales tax, of which the indirect taxes seem to have played a considerable role in financing development, but have also generated undesirable results in the economy in terms of adversely affecting the costs, prices and incentives.[3] The other important sources of domestic resource mobilization are the earnings of the parastatals (government enterprises), and the banking and insurance system. While the experience of public enterprise has been quite unsatisfactory in terms of generating surpluses, the system of banking has been alleged to be least conducive in terms of promoting the goals of development finance and in providing incentives to capital formation. The economy, therefore, has been characterized by limited achievement under economic planning, without the much needed transformation from traditional society to modernism, industrialization and diversification. We will now examine some of these aspects.

Most of the goods relating to the basic necessities, semi-luxuries, and others are not manufactured domestically, and the installed industrial capacities generally relate to intermediate goods and some capital goods. The locally produced cement, beer, fertilizer, shoes, tyres, iron sheets, and textiles reflect capacity underutilization for reasons of supply constraints such as the lack of suitable investments for production, expansion, diversification, and for reasons of inadequate demand arising out of lower incomes, lower quality and standardization, lack of awareness and knowledge, and general poverty, apart from other reasons.

The goods generally imported and associated with lower and middle income groups are cooking oils, cooking gas, bread, aerated drinks, dairy products, cloth, soap, plastics, blades, batteries, radios, detergents, farm implements, aluminium ware, tooth paste, tooth brush, cigarettes, insecticides, and drugs and chemicals. The durable consumer goods associated with middle and upper income groups are building materials, iron and steel, nylon, paints, plastic emulsions, corrugated sheets, cables and wires, hardware, tyres and tubes, domestic appliances, and electricals and electronics.

The economy faces the problem of supply shortages given the general dependence on imports, and lags in international transportation. The problem would be more serious because of real and artificial shortages, uncertainties, hoarding, stocking, and black marketing, and because of in-availability of locally manufactured substitutes. With the frequent revision of prices of goods sold, and increased indirect taxation, the Tanzanian market behaviour and the consumer psychology had been anything but conducive to the requirements of development and stability. There appears to be considerable decline in the purchasing power of the people leading to a decline in the standards of living and levels of efficiency, under conditions of persistent inflation. We have to therefore, examine the nature of the tax system, cost of living, and the wage policy, so as to throw light on related matters.

**The Tax System of Tanzania**

A brief examination of the behaviour of the key taxes may be made in order to indicate the nature of their burden, before the related matters are examined. The rates of *personal income tax* in Tanzania became steeply progressive in the year 1974 itself, and the requirements of augmenting greater revenues for development made the 1980 Act even more progressive. The effective tax rate was 13.9 per cent in 1974, 14.8 per cent in 1979 and 17.6 per cent in 1980. The effect of tax rates on the higher ranges is much more pronounced, and the top salaries were revised only once in 1974 after 1966. Their effective tax rate of 17.2 per cent in 1968 rose to 25.7 per cent in 1972, and to 28.1 per cent in 1974, while the money earnings remained constant. In 1980, the effective tax rate for this group was increased to 31.1 per cent. The tax system has no concessions in computing taxable income, except the nominal allowance given for the number of children of the tax payer.

Revenue from *corporate income tax* depends on the profit of companies under both public and private sectors, and the parastatal (public) sector of Tanzania has grown by leaps and bounds with the increasing trend of nationalization. The tax rate of corporate income tax has been revised to 45 per cent for resident companies, and 50 per cent for non-resident companies in the year 1979-80. The net profits of the pubic sector companies have grown steadily, but declined from 1979-80, in spite of the increase in the total income (Table 1.5) while the public sector is not known for profiteering, the private sector does not seem to have grown in terms of expansions and starting of new firms, given the effect of corporate income taxation.

*Import Duties* are based on the value of imports. The share of the import duties in the total tax revenue was 38.8 per cent in 1968-69, 25 per cent in 1972-73, and 7.3 per cent in 1976-77 and 16 per cent in 1978-79. Low import capacity, and the basis of tax being specific in nature are some of the reasons for the inability of the government to increase revenue on this account.

*Export tax* is related to the primary agricultural commodities, namely, coffee, cotton, cashewnuts, tea, pyrethrum extracts, timber and sisal. The share of this tax as a proportion to the total ranged from 4.1 per cent in 1969-70 to 8.3 per cent in 1973-74, 10 per cent in 1977-78, and 7.5 per cent in 1978-79. This tax seems to have had fewer discretionary changes compared to the changes made in respect of import duties. The specific tax rate on some items has been converted into *ad valorem* with effect from 1977-78, resulting in a remarkable increase in revenue.

*Sales tax* relates to a wide range of goods. The share of the tax was 16.9 per cent in 1970-71 and 41.5 per cent in 1978-79. According to the Finance Minister, it was designed to provide a sound and reliable long run source of Government revenue to replace most of the local taxes which were found difficult to collect and too costly to administer. The tax was subjected to discretionary changes almost every year, and the government has come to rely heavily on this source.

The *excise duties* are levied on about twenty locally manufactured goods, and a large share of tax revenue accrues from cigarettes, sugar, beer, and fabrics. Tobacco and cigarettes are taxed on *ad valorem,* and the others on the basis of specific duties. Production in the economy as such has had a set back since the mid 1970's due to foreign exchange shortages, lack of skilled manpower, and raw material shortages. The revenue from excises had fallen with the fall in production and the fall in the value of manufacture. (Table 1.6). The rates of excises range from 30 to 55 per cent and with little diversification and change in the quality of the products, the level of taxation is felt least desirable. Excise duty on soaps is at 55 per cent per kilogram, sugar at 46 per cent per kilogram, and textiles at 30 per cent per square metre. The prices of most commodities are found to be relatively on the high side given the influence of (a) customs duty levied on a number of items imported and exported, so as to preserve the interest of local manufactures, and (b) the sales tax, which is being used world-wide, more as a revenue device than as a measure of stabilization, in spite of the fact that it has the potential to fall on the regressive side, affect productivity adversely, and add to the price level. And it is often true that, during the decades of development, the people have generally a greater preference for consumer goods after the basic needs are met, and therefore, taxes associated with consumer goods are most likely to erode the incomes of the major sections of the society.

**Elasticity of Taxes**

As regards the elasticity of taxes, export tax has the highest elasticity, followed by sales tax and corporate tax, and the import tax has been inelastic. Export tax has grown with the increase in the price of export commodities, particularly coffee, cotton and cashewnuts, but, over time, it should be observed that their competitiveness may be hit at international levels, which have not grown in a period of development. For instance, the value of exports has been 4706 sh. mill in 1981, 4144 sh. mill in 1982, 4138 sh. mill in 1983, 5761 sh. mill in 1984, and 4960 sh. mill in 1986. The elasticity of sales tax has been mainly due to the increase in the production of sales tax and textiles, and beer, and due to enhanced *ad valorem* tax rates. The elasticity of corporate income tax has been attributed to the favourable performance of some manufacturing, financial and commercial sectors. The inelasticity of individual income tax may be attributed to the fact that the income of people who are in the higher tax-paying bracket had almost remained constant for the past many years. As regards the import tax, the inelasticity may be due to the composition of imports and the nature of tax rates. The relative importance of the heavily taxed items has declined over the years due to foreign exchange constraint and protection given to local manufactures, and the tax rate has been on specific lines rather than *ad valorem*. The excise tax has been found to be inelastic, due to the declining trend in the output of the commodity. The tax system as a whole is found to be fairly inelastic due to low elasticities of some important items.[4]

Indirect taxes as such, in the context of Tanzania, may be said to be incapable of achieving the multiple objectives such as stability, productivity, and progressivity, for more than one reason, i.e., (a) the economy is not poised to achieve the level of diversification and buoyancy needed, (b) the incomes have been low and stagnant over the years as well as in relative terms, (c) the taxes merely add to the level of prices of the goods and serve the immediate purpose they are designed for, i.e., to augment tax revenue, and (d) the tax structure has not attained the level of sophistication necessary to combine multiple objectives. The result, however, has been that the tax revenues and prices have grown faster, even faster than the growth in wages and incomes, and with the erosion in the real wages, the fall in the standards of living has been an inevitable concomitant of the whole process. We may now, therefore, examine the question of cost of living, wage and price indices, in a period development.

*Cost of living, wages, and wage revisions:* The index of retail prices for goods consumed by minimum wage earners with 1969 as the base, has gone up from 93.0 in 1966 to 107.4 in 1971, 306.7 in 1976, and to 512.2 in 1980, for all goods. For food items for these years, it was 98.2, 108.5, 323.0 and 460.1 (Table 1.3).

**Table 1.1 :** *Zero Order Correlation Matrix*

| | *P* | *M* | *IT* | *W* |
|---|---|---|---|---|
| P | 1.000 | 0.9699 | 0.9872 | 0.9390 |
| M | | 1.0000 | 0.9870 | 0.8946 |
| IT | | | 1.0000 | 0.9485 |
| W | | | | 1.0000 |

The cost of living index for goods consumed by urban Tanzania has gone up from 98.1 in 1968 to 116.7 in 1972, to 194.3 in 1975, and to 382.4 in 1980. The cost of living index for goods consumed by middle income groups has gone up from 96.4 in 1967 to 102.0 in 1972, to 225.7 in 1975 and to 425.6 in 1980. And for upper income groups, it has gone up from 90.8 in 1966 to 113.8 in 1971, to 233.5 in 1976, and to 416.3 in 1980.

The avowed policy of wages in Tanzania has been that, wage revisions reflect only the essential requisites of living, and that "the wage structure for the economy as a whole, ove. a period of time, should reflect considerable compression and equality between the grades, occupations, groups classes and functional entities." During the period 1960 to 1976, wage revisions were made five times. Under the Colonial rule, the urban minimum wage was raised from 49 sh per month in 1960 to 107.50 sh, i.e., an increase of 120 per cent. In 1961, it was increased from 107.50 sh to 130 sh, and two years later, revised to 150 sh, and to 1970 sh in 1969. In 1972, it was revised to 240 sh, to 340 in 1974, and to 380 sh in 1975. The minimum wage in 1975 was 124 per cent higher than in 1963. In 1980, it was revised to 480 sh, and to 600 sh in 1983, keeping in mind, the significant erosion in the real incomes.

**Table 1.2 :** *Estimated Values of the Parameters of the Regression Equations*

| *Functional form* | *a* | $b_1$ | $b_2$ | $b_3$ | $R_{-2}$ | *F* | *DW* |
|---|---|---|---|---|---|---|---|
| $\log p = \log a + b_1 \log M$ | −1.9306 | 0.8763* (17.5373) | | | 0.9623* | 307.5564 | 1.1104 |
| $\log p = \text{lag}\ a + b_1 \log IT$ | −1.6008 | 0.9023* (15.2104) | | | 0.9505* | 231.35 | 0.8510 |
| $\log p = \log a + b_1 \log M + b_2 \log IT$ | −1.8743 | 0.5980** (2.1101) | 0.2928 (0.9977) | | 0.9623* | 154.21 | 1.0586 |
| $\log p = \log a + b_1 \log M + b_2 \log IT + b_3 \log W$ | −3.2579 | 0.7189** (2.1905) | −0.0528 (0.0986) | 0.3873 (0.7788) | 0.9608* | 98.96 | 1.2574 |

* Significant at 1 per cent level.

** Significant at 5 per cent level.

Figures in the parenthesis are t-values.

**Table 1.3 :** *Minimum Wage, Retail Price, and Real Wage Index*

| *Year* | *Minimum Wage (Urban) Rs.* | *Retail Price Index* 1969-100 | *Real Minimum Wage Index* 1969-100 |
|---|---|---|---|
| 1963 | 150 | 80.0 | 100.0 |
| 1964 | 150 | 82.0 | 107.3 |
| 1965 | 150 | 88.8 | 99.1 |
| 1966 | 150 | 93.0 | 94.6 |
| 1967 | 150 | 95.4 | 92.2 |
| 1968 | 150 | 98.9 | 87.0 |
| 1969 | 170 | 99.7 | 100.0 |
| 1970 | 170 | 103.7 | 96.1 |
| 1971 | 170 | 107.4 | 92.8 |
| 1972 | 240 | 118.6 | 118.7 |
| 1973 | 240 | 129.3 | 108.9 |
| 1974 | 340 | 169.0 | 118.0 |
| 1975 | 380 | 248.5 | 89.7 |
| 1976 | 340 | 306.7 | 72.7 |
| 1977 | 380 | 358.4 | 62.2 |
| 1978 | 380 | 418.7 | 56.5 |
| 1979 | 380 | 437.3 | 50.4 |
| 1980 | 480 | 512.2 | 41.3 |

**Source :** Compiled from *The Economic Survey* 1981, and *Survey of Employment and Earnings*, 1973-74 and 1977-78, Government of Tanzania.

The government and the parastatals together constitute the biggest employers of the economy, and the latter accounts for the major share of the wage bill, particularly due to the larger employment potential under the industrial units of the parastatals, compared to agriculture. However, it is to be pointed out that, while the wages and prices have registered increases, the index of real wages had eroded more than ten times due to inflation.

Employment is also provided in sizeable numbers in the private sector and in the informal sector, where the returns to capital are generally more attractive, particularly in such areas as hotels, handicrafts, fishing, baking, meat and poultry, forest products, hides and skins, and transportation of goods and passengers. Also, this is

**Table 1.4 :** *Tax Revenue, Wage Bill and GDP of Tanzania (1969-81)*

*(Millions of shillings)*

| Year | *Wage Bill* | *Wage Bill as a % of Total GDP* | *Total Tax Revenue* | *Total Tax Revenue as a % of Total GDP* | *GDP of Industrial Origin* | *GDP of Agricultural Origin* |
|---|---|---|---|---|---|---|
| 1969 | 1384.7 | (19.08) | 1169.5 | (16.11) | 4170.0 | 3089.0 |
| 1970 | 1501.7 | (19.55) | 1354.6 | (17.64) | 4475.0 | 3205.0 |
| 1971 | 1589.9 | (19.87) | ·1466.7 | (18.33) | 4835.0 | 3166.0 |
| 1972 | 1689.9 | (19.79) | 1915.1 | (22.43) | 514.0 | 3425.0 |
| 1973 | 2155.5 | (24.49) | 2593.9 | (29.48) | 5342.0 | 3458.0 |
| 1974 | 3213.6 | (35.63) | 3298.1 | (36.56) | 5705.0 | 3315.0 |
| 1975 | 3260.0 | (34.15) | 3867.4 | (40.52) | 5910.0 | 3828.0 |
| 1976 | 3309.1 | (32.86) | 4436.6 | (44.06) | 6122.0 | 3947.0 |
| 1977 | 3664.1 | (34.36) | 5461.3 | (51.22) | 6419.0 | 4244.0 |
| 1978 | 3708.1 | (32.93) | 5992.3 | (53.22) | 6700.0 | 4560.0 |
| 1979 | 4286.2 | (37.96) | 6614.0 | (58.58) | 6914.0 | 4377.0 |
| 1980 | 4291.7 | (37.12) | 7729.0 | (66.85) | 7207.0 | 4354.0 |
| 1981 | 5003.6 | (44.88) | 8242.0 | (73.93) | 7125.0 | 4024.0 |

**Source :** *The Economic Surveys* of the Government of Tanzania.

an important sector which represents a flourishing source of black incomes and speculation, and potentially dangerous in terms of generating inflation.

## The Financial Superstructure

In the financing of investments needed for development, the financial superstructure of a country has an important role as the financial intermediary for mobilising the savings, and help hold assets in financial rather than in physical form, as a necessary condition of economic development. The existing system of banking in Tanzania is a result of the Arusha Declaration (1967) and the consequent nationalization of the expatriate financial entities. The Central Bank of the nation, i.e., the Bank of Tanzania at the apex, and the National Bank of Commerce representing all commercial operations after the merger of banks into it, and the Tanzania Investment Bank, The Tanzania Rural Development, and the Tanzania Housing Bank, represent the three specialized functions.

In addition, the two institutions, i.e., the National Insurance Corporation, and the National Provident Fund, organise the insurance business; while the latter mobilises forced savings from government and other employees, for being invested in government bonds and stocks. While the Bank of Tanzania organizes the monetary management of the country, the commercial banking system, the Insurance Corporation, and the Provident Fund account for the bulk of savings mobilization in deposit and other forms. But there seems to be much to be desired in the operations of these independent systems which have imbibed all the qualities of monopolies, with the exception of motivating themselves to productivity and participation.[5] These units have been alleged to be prolific in their checks, controls, bureaucratic delays, and inefficiency, resulting from rapid rate of recruitment of the personnel, absence of material and moral incentives in employment and the effect of the rampant inflation.[6] Also, these institutions are "financially ill-equipped" because their major source for funds and business is the government, which is the final authority for internal and external finances. "Since they have to pay high interest rates and other service charges on funds borrowed externally, they naturally end up changing even higher interest rates to their clients in Tanzania as a necessary evil for the use of funds. It is to be noted that the deposit rate has been 4 per cent upto 1984, 4.50 in 1985, 8.50 in 1986, 17.50 in 1987 and 1988; while the lending rate has been 12 per cent in 1981 and 1982, 13 per cent upto 1986, 18.50 per cent in 1986, 29.50 per cent in 1987 and 1988".[7] And most investments are made in the relatively inefficient government sector by the National Bank of Commerce, while the need for investing in private activities and industrialization is not yet realised.

As the banks are totally averse to accepting the savings deposits of expatriates, and as the other depositers face the problem of being questioned as to the source of income, and as a great deal of funds exist in unlicensed "private banks", the efficiency of the present financial intermediaries in mobilizing domestic savings is highly questionable. In addition, the currency ratio, i.e., the ratio of currency in circulation to money supply, being very high (at 40 per cent in 1983) and given the inflation, the public's portfolio preference for cash has been very high, reflecting the nature of day to day well being, the faith of the people in the banking system, and the level of monetization of the backward economy. The much recent restriction of the Bank of Tanzania is that the expatriates are entitled to only current accounts at zero rate of interest even on legally earned incomes.[8] And with inflation at about 30 per cent, the real rate of interest has been almost negative since 1975, the banking system has to do a great deal more on the lines of revising the interest rates for attracting deposits.[9]

We have so far indicated the nature of reliance of the government on domestic resource mobilisation for financing the development needs, the nature of decline in the standards of living, and the inadequacy of wage revisions to compensate for the rapidly falling real incomes, and the inability of the government to keep the prices under control with the help of taxes, given the existence of the prive and the informal sector, which provides the safety volve for the much needed additional money incomes through various prosperous but concealed avenues compared to the organized ones. It has been observed that, "the employees are forced to supplement their incomes through engaging in illicit market activities, work part-time, use office facilities for own ends, and engage in other income generating activities, and show an enormous drift and preference for fringe benefits."[10]

**The Development Perspectives**

We may now examine whether the expansion in the government activity and the efforts to planning for development have helped the economy to promote growth and stability. The development strategy of Tanzania was generally clouded by inflation, low rates of growth in the key sectors, low levels of capital formation, and unfavourable balance of payments. Droughts and other forms of natural disasters have often overtaken the modest attempts of progress. Cocoa, sisal and coffee the most important export crops provided the main steam for economic progress under the colonial rule, and after they were taken over, the inability of the economy to maintain production and compete internationally, has largely affected the availability of investible resources.[11] Industrial development was badly affected due to input shortages, particularly foreiegn exchange, resulting in capacity underutilization of significant level.[12]

However, the development policy generally reiterates that resources would be properly utilized, agriculture stabilized, bring about structural transformation in industry, promote the production of basic items such as iron and steel and chemicals, and thereby promote the other goals of the economy such as faster sectoral growth rates.

But the results in the first five year plan (1964-69), and the second five year plan (1969-74) did not indicate any encouraging trend in the development process. The increase in the GDP was aimed at 6.7 per cent in the first plan, and the per capita income was estimated to increase at 4 per cent, and the result was 5 per cent and 2.3 per cent respectively. The growth in the Second Plan was lower than in the first plan at 4.8 per cent. During the two annual plans in 1974-75 and 1975-75, the increase in GDP was 4.6 and 5.2 per cent respectively. The Third Plan (Table 1.5) (1976-81) estimated the increase at 6.75 per cent, with 5.1 for agriculture, 9.3 for mining, 9.3 for industry, 10.3 for water and electricity, 6.4 for workers, 6.5 for transport and communications,

**Table 1.5 :** *Corporate Taxation, Profits and Income of Parastatals*

| *Year* | *Revenue from Corporate Income Taxation (m. Shs.)* | *Net Profits from Parastatals (m. Shs.)* | *Total Income of the Parastatals (m. Shs.)* |
|---|---|---|---|
| 1969-70 | 149.3 | 220.1 | 2457.9 |
| 1970-71 | 137.4 | 279.2 | 3200.8 |
| 1971-72 | 196.7 | 409.3 | 3706.1 |
| 1972-73 | 248.4 | 501.0 | 4633.9 |
| 1973-74 | 272.8 | 626.3 | 5869.4 |
| 1974-75 | 364.1 | 730.4 | 8373.1 |
| 1975-76 | 366.3 | 855.9 | 9557.2 |
| 1976-77 | 557.6 | 1000.8 | 10457.2 |
| 1977-78 | 832.7 | 1492.7 | 11488.3 |
| 1978-79 | 1023.3 | 2003.9 | 15568.0 |
| 1979-80 | 1407.0 | 808.0 | 19568.0 |
| 1980-81 | 1301.0 | 458.1 | 20525.0 |

**Source :** *The Economic Surveys of the Government of Tanzania.*

**Table 1.6 :** *Quantities of Main Excisable Commodities*

| | *1969* | *1971* | *1973* | *1976* | *1978* |
|---|---|---|---|---|---|
| Beer (litre) | 20,424,820 | 44,855,997 | 69,383,578 | 54,180,760 | 27,886,163 |
| Sugar (Kg.) | 1,819,703 | 1,013,343 | 959,962 | 810,285 | 1,190,571 |
| Cigarette (000) | 2,771,610 | 2,871,106 | 3,309,176 | 2,960,573 | 2,013,211 |
| Fabrics | 58,316,657 | 56,154,195 | 78,595,400 | 59,070,820 | 52,965,402 |
| Manufactured Tobacco (Kg.) | 13,324 | 3,188 | 5,904 | 1,747 | 1,046 |

**Source :** Annual Trade Reports of Kenya, Uganda and Tanzania 1969-76.
*Tanzania Annual Trade Report* - Custom and Excise Department 1977-79.

**Table 1.7 :** *Elasticity of Tax Structure (1968-79)*

| | *Constant* | *Elasticity* | $R^2$ | *Rate of Taxation* |
|---|---|---|---|---|
| Total Tax Revenue | –0.074 | 0.825 (5.00) | 0.97 | 0.184 |
| Income Tax | 0.654 | 0.685 (8.00) | 0.93 | 0.410 |
| Corporation Income Tax | 0.966 | 1.108 (4.20) | 0.94 | 0.266 |
| Export Tax | –7.438 | 2.818 (5.68) | 0.89 | 0.245 |
| Import Tax | 1.437 | 0.338 (3.10) | 0.37 | 0.038 |
| Sales Tax | –1.498 | 1.058 (7.15) | 0.86 | 0.065 |
| Excise Duties | 1.686 | 0.210 (1.00) | 0.18 | 0.041 |

**Notes :** (1) All the elasticity coefficients except item 7, are found to be statistically significant at 1 per cent level of significance. (2) For item 1, the independent variable is GDP. For item 2, the independent variable is taxable income. For item 3, the independent variable is profits of the undertakings and government establishments. For item 4, the independent variable is value of exports. For item 5, the independent variable is value of imports. For item 6, the independent variable is the share of private expenditure on textiles, beer, soft drinks, and cigarettes, which account for 90 per cent of revenue from sales tax, and for item 6, the independent variable is the value of output of beer, sugar and cigarettes, which constitutes 90 per cent of the excise duty. (3) The sources of data are (*a*) National Accounts of Tanzania, (*b*) Economic Bulletin of the Bank of Tanzania, (*c*) Income Tax Statistics of the Bureau of Statistics, and (d) the Economic Survey, (4) the regression results are cited from an earlier unpublished study made at he University of Dar-es-Salaam.

and 5.6 for others, keeping in mind the ability to borrow and the surpluses in question for financing a plan nearly three times bigger than the Second Plan.[13]

The cost of government administration has grown with the growth of public enterprise activity, and the expenditure on wages, salaries, rents, fringe benefits and other costs have risen so much that the activities such as social services including education, health, hospitals, community and extension services, housing, water and urban services have received lower priority. The least productive items, namely, the cost of administration, defence, and servicing the public debt, occupy the maximum attention of the current budgets. At the same time, the indiscriminate public enterprise activity has led to overall declines in factor productivity, and any productivity gains that could be expected seem to have been dissipated in additional employment rather than augmenting gross parastatal surpluses.

**Table 1.8 :** *The Third Plan Sectoral Development Finance*

*(Percentages to total)*

| | *Government Development Budget* | *Estimated Parastatal Revenue* | *Sectoral Distribution of capital investment* |
|---|---|---|---|
| Agriculture | 11.50 | 14.18 | 12.35 |
| Live-stock | 2.04 | 3.43 | 2.34 |
| Natural Resources | 1.35 | 0.04 | 1.54 |
| Mining | 3.54 | 3.06 | 3.42 |
| Industry | 24.20 | 35.91 | 26.68 |
| Commerce and Tourism | 1.23 | 5.15 | 2.14 |
| Water | 6.82 | 0.42 | 5.46 |
| Building and Construction | 9.92 | 9.97 | 9.93 |
| Power | 4.74 | 0.05 | 5.01 |
| Communication and Transport | 7.26 | 11.56 | 8.17 |
| Education | 7.94 | 0.52 | 6.37 |
| Health | 3.47 | 0.07 | 2.88 |
| Administration | 15.42 | 8.66 | 13.71 |

**Source :** *The Third Five Year Plan*, Government to Tanzania.

The increasing government activity has also transformed the government as the chief consumer of the economy since about the mid 70's when the current expenditures increased by 150 per cent. The ratio of consumption expenditures to total current expenditures increased from about 65 per cent to 86 per cent. The explosive increase in government consumption expenditures is due to (a) the decentralization of the government made in 1972 which has absorbed the former local governments in the accounting frame of the Central Government which had increased its responsibilities by increasing the number of employees by 65000 from a base of about one lakh, particularly among senior and middle level jobs, (b) increased wages and salaries on a dramatic scale far exceeding the impressive increases in tax revenues, and (c) the increase in the prices of all goods and services consequent to increases in money supply over and above planned levels, as well as costly imports which are crucial to the very existence of the economy.

It has been observed that development finance had faced a pattern of overcommitment of ambitious social and economic targets, leading to closing down or partial utilization and completion of projects, at a great cost to the economy, and a Report of the World Bank warns that such pattern of overcommitment be reversed, and that fewer investment ventures have to be entertained consistent with financial availability and productivity.

**The Recent Economic Situation**

Interestingly, the Tanzania Basic Economic Report of the World Bank, however, considered that, given the general situation, the performance of tax and fiscal policies were satisfactory and that the prospects for the economy were sound, and if the policy priorities were brought into effect, "the real GDP can be expected to grow at about 6 per cent per year during the decade of the 1980s, the living standards of the rural masses will improve by some 30 per cent by 1990 (compared to 1976), poverty will be contained and much improved performances on savings and exports will brings the economy close to the objectives of self reliance."[14]

Given the experience of the 1970's, the above reaction may have to be termed one of supreme complacency, of the economy started facing much more serious handicaps and alarming failures in about the year 1975 itself. We may now trace the recent experience in this regard.

The revenue deficits of the Government have been 3667 mill sh in 1981, 5512 in 1982, 4333 in 1983, 4414 in 1984, and 6802 in 1985. In this period, public expenditure has risen form 14755 m.sh in 1981 to 28508 m.sh in 1985. Government consumption has more than doubled from 6105 m.sh in 1981 to 12447 m.sh in 1986. The G.D.P. has been nearly stagnant at 41654 m. sh in 1981, 42192 m.sh in 1982, 42008 m.sh in 1983, 43049 in 1984, and 42952 m.sh in 1985, at 1980 prices. Export earnings have been around 6000 m.sh in the entire period, while the inputs have risen from 10162 m.sh in 1981 to 17480 m.sh in 1985. While the export earnings constituted 14580 m.sh in 1986, the imports were at 37026 m.sh. The deficit in the trade balance has been 372.2 m.sh in 1981, 539 in 1982, 333 in 1983, 385 in 1984, 532 in 1985, and 566 m. US $ in 1986.[15]

The consumer price index indicates (with 1980 as its base) that it has increased by more than six times from 125.6 in 1981 to 162.0 in 1982, 205.8 in 1983, 278.6 in 1984, 373.6 in 1985, 494.6 in 1986, and 642.7 in 1987. This index is almost in step with the money supply in the economy which has risen form 15401 m.sh in 1981 to 18323 in 1982, to 20564 in 1983, to 20608 in 1984, to 25514 in 1985, and to 35810 in 1986. And alongside, the government consumption has also increased, as observed earlier, due to the fact that it has been the biggest employer both directly and on account of the public enterprises, indicating the rising magnitude of the wage bill of the government.

Thus, an analysis of the case of Tanzania, over a period of two development decades points out that, the public activity has increased since the time the nation achieved its political dependence. But the efficieney of the economy suffered at several levels. With the exist of private foreign enterprise, the key plantations which maintained the entire economy at one time as the chief export crops, have now received a set back in terms of production and productivity under the auspices of government management, where the production incentives and managerial efficiency have been inadequate, and therefore, the exports have suffered quantitatively and in terms of international competition. The economy is forced to depend on resources financed by taxation which requires to be rationalised in terms of its suitability to mop up the required resources without affecting the basic incentives and consumption levels of the poorer masses.[16] The tax system requires to be made income elastic by imparting progressivity in the tax rates, and by expanding the bases of taxation, so as to reduce the burden on lower income groups. The indirect taxes have to show greater diversification so as to use them not merely for augmenting revenues, but to serve the question of larger interests of the society such as capital formation, better income distribution, progress in standards of living, controlling of inflationary pressures, and furthering the levels of production. Under the expanding government and parastatal sector, the employment has grown and the wage bill has also grown. The prices in the economy have grown faster than the wages resulting in a steep fall in the standards of living, and inflation has added to the general misery of the economy in terms of speculation, distorted economic and social values, and widening of income disparities. The much desired transformation in the economy from agriculture to industrialization did not come about in a long period of time due to the inability of the government to finance outlays consistent with sectoral requirements. The capacities created in basic and heavy industry at the cost of continuous import commitments, could not be utilized properly.[17] The financial superstructure created with the nationalization of all commercial banks, and the creation of Investment Bank and Rural Development Bank have not served the purpose for which they were established due to the fact that productivity of the financial superstructure has fallen and with the freezing of salaries and abolition of material incentives, the question of reviving the incentives, and revitalising the bureaucracy would be a difficult prospect. And the savings mobilised by the banking system, given the rate of inflation and the structure of interest rates, and the banking regulations, are totally inadequate to finance development. The deficits of the government have been consistently higher, and the losses of the parastatals have been significant. The imports have been so very necessitated and crucial that the economy has to import consumer goods, intermediate goods as well as basic goods, and face a chronic deficit in the balance of payments position. And given the supply constraints in the form of technical dependence on foreign capital, inadequate infrastructure, and inability of the government to mitigate the imbalances generated by colonial rule, it takes a long time for this country to promote development consistent with times.

The impasse has been faced by the economy for too long a period and before a total atrophy sets into the body politic, it will have to steer itself out of the present policies. In the first instance the economy has to make an attempt to commercialise itself on the strength of individual and local incentives. These may be restituted only on the basis of suitable and realistic wage and price policies with the help of rationalistic tax policies with suitable protection to real incomes to safeguard standards of living from a run away inflation. It would be necessary to reduce government and parastatal activity of the wasteful type, and promote the private sector with suitable privatization based on commercial lines and rational employment policies. The government has a responsibility to promote the faith and confidence of the people in the banking system as to effect greater domestic resource mobilization at optimal rates of interest, and arrange to invest funds on productive lines, with the help of financial liberalization and relaxation of controls. The participation levels of the international financing units and private foreign investment do not match the present requirements of capital base necessary for economic transformation, nor will the question of speedy technological transfer be solved, unless the required changes are brought about in all important economic and social policies.

**Appendix**

For examining the impact of money supply, indirect taxes and wage bill on prices, the following regression model is estimated by the method of Least Squares

$$\log P = a + b_1 \log M$$

$$\log P = a + b_1 \log IT$$

$$\log P = a + b_1 \log M + b_2 \log IT$$

$$\log P = a + b_1 \log M + b_2 \log IT + b_3 \log W$$

where P = is the price level

M is the money supply

IT is the indirect taxes

W is the wage bill

a,b's are the parameters

Zero order correlation coefficients of the variables included in the regression show that there is a very high correlation between money supply and indirect taxes, money supply and wage bill and indirect taxes and wage bill. So including these three variables in the regression presents multi collinearily problem. Therefore, these variable are considered separately. Regression results presented in Table 1.2 indicate that when the price variable is regressed separately on money supply and indirect taxes, the coefficients are statistically significant at one per cent level and have expected signs. The money supply elasticity of the price level 0.8763 and indirect taxes elasticity of the price level is 0.9023. Money supply explains 96 per cent of the variation in the price level and indirect taxes explains 95 per cent of the variation in price level. When the price level is regressed on both money supply and indirect taxes, the regression coefficients have expected signs but only the coefficient of money supply is statistically significant. It may be due to the presence of multicollinearity. These two variables together explain 96 per cent of the variation in the price level. When the wage bill is also added to the set of independent variables there is no improvement in the value of $R^{-2}$. The coefficient of money supply alone is significant. The coefficient of indirect taxes does not have the expected sign. It may also be due to the presence of multicollinearity.

The analysis reveals that money supply and indirect taxes separately and together explain 96 per cent of the variation in the price level. The wage factor does not seem to be an important one in view of the fact that there is wage freeze in the economy. The results confirm the *apriori* expectation that indirect taxes are inflationary in their effects and money supply does influence the price level *a la* quantity theory.[18]

The results would have been more clear and forthright had the data series relate to a much longer period and changes in variables are considered rather than their absolute magnitudes. Inflation is such a complicated phenomenon that it is influenced by a host of quantifiable and non-quantifiable factors, and therefore, the present analysis of inflation has taken into account only broad determinants.

## REFERENCES

1. D. Rwegasira made a study of inflation and instability in Tanzania in his paper "Inflation and Monetary expansion", in Kwan S. Kim, Robert B. Mabele and Michael J. Schultheis, (ed), *Papers on The Political Economy of Tanzania*, 1979.

2. For an analysis of the Growing public sector, see Ann Seidman, *Planning for Development in Sub-Saharan Africa*, 1974, pp. 136-146.

3. For a study of the limits of direct taxation, and the increasing role of indirect taxation in financing development, see Winfried Manig, "Government Capacity of Levying Taxes in Peripheral Countries", *Economic*, edited by the *Institute of Scientific Cooperation*, Tubingen, Vol. 27, pp. 61-89.

4. The results of regression analysis are given in table 8 with details of dependent and independent variables and the sources of data.

5. Mukwanason Hyuha, "The Financial Superstructure in Tanzania : Prospects and Problems", in L.A. Msambichaka and S. Chandrasekhar (ed.), *Readings of Economic Policy of Tanzania, Economic Research Bureau* of University of

Dares-Salaam, 1984, Also, for a critique of the existing super-structure of the financial system of Tanzania, see Amon J. Nsekela, *The NBC and National Economy in the 1980's*, Address to UDSM Finance Association, 1982.

6. Nsekela, Op. cit., It is observed that "the NBC also suffers from productivity problems. In this respect it is not different from other public sector institutions. The Virtual abolition of material incentives in the early 1970's, the failing to replace them with any political or 'moral' incentives and the subsequent relative freezing of salaries in the context of rising prices has, inevitably, resulted in reduced productivity," pp. 6-7.

7. *International Financial Statistics*, 1988, pp. 502-505.

8. Hyuha, (1984), Op. cit.

9. Hyuha (1984), observes that "the country's domestic resources even if they were mobilised or exploited to the maximum, are far inadequate in relation to the resources needed for development." Also, "the interest rate payable on savings deposits was about 2.5 per cent in 1936, it moved to about 4 per cent in the 1960's and is now about 7.5 per cent in this country. Meanwhile, inflation is well over 30 per cent at present. Hence, the real rate of interest has been negative almost since 1975. In so far as savings may be sensitive not only to the level of income but also to interest rates, these rate need a rapid upward movement. Financial repression may not be advantageous to this country. Thus, there is need to study the structure of interest rates in the country with a view to evolve an 'optimal' structure." Also, see Hyuha, Financial Intermediaries and Economic Growth in Developing Countries", *Journal of Economic Reflections*, Vol. II, No. 1, 1982.

10. Theodore R. Valentine, "Wage adjustments, progressive tax rates, and accelerated inflation : Issues of equity in the wage sector of Tanzania", *Economic Research Bureau Seminar Paper*, August 16, 1983, University of Dar-es-Salaam.

11. L.A. Msambichaka, "Agricultural Development in Tanzania : Problems and Priorities", in L.A. *Msambichaka and S. Chandrasekhar*, ed., Op. cited., pp. 44-67.

12. S.M. Wangwe, "The Industrial Development Experience : Some Structural Imbalances", in L.A. *Msambichaka and S. Chandrasekhar*, ed., Op. cited., pp. 21-29.

13. B.J. Ndulu, "Investment Patterns and Impacts in the Post-Arusha Tanzania : 1970-80", in L.A. *Msambichaka and S. Chandrasekhar*, Op. cit., pp. 1-21.

14. *The Tanzania Basic Economic Report, World Bank*, Report No. 1616-TA, December, 1977, para 36.

15. *International Financial Statistics*, Op. cit.

16. Yukon Huang, "Distribution of Tax Burden in Tanzania", *Economic Journal*, March 1976. It is observed that "in future, extraction of additional resources in excess of those provided by income growth will be a very difficult process, politically more so than economically,". "It must therefore be on the expenditure side that improvements are made." Also, see J. Loxley, "The Finance of Government spending in Tanzania since Independnce", Raslimali, 1974, *Tanzania Investment Bank*, pp. 22-25; Loxley, "Government recurrent revenue in Tanzania", *Institute of Financial Management Papers*, September, 1974.

17. Samuel M. Wangwe. "Industrialization and Resources Allocation in a Developing Economy : The Case of Recent Experiences in Tanzania", *World Development*. Vol. II. No. 6. 1983. pp. 483-492.

18. Rwegasira (1979) pointed out that "the inadequacy of the money supply variables for explaining price movements during the period necessitates further analysis if the nature of inflation is to be better understood." opp. p. 152. The present study indicates the influence of money supply on price level, and also emphasizes that indirect taxes have a role in cost escalation in the economy.

# 2

# Employment and Wages in Tanzanian Parastatals

The purpose of this analysis to trace the growth of parastatal activity in Tanzania since the Arusha Declaration of 1967 and examine the nature of increase in employment, wages and productivity and their relationships. The role of the parastatal[1] sector has expanded greatly since the Arusha Declaration, which brought about the nationalisation of Banking and Insurance Companies, and the enactment of Industrial shares (acquisition) Act. As a result of this, the share of the government ownership in the industrial sector had widely increased. There were only about 43 known parastatal enterprises prior to 1967, compared with 73 in 1968, 117 in 1973, 149 in 1977 and about 400 in 1983, due to the fact that government has emerged as the chief producer and distributor of all the important economic activities. Thus, Tanzania seems to have made tremendous efforts to accelerate the tempo of industrial and subsidiary activities.

The activities of the parastatals are briefly as follows. The agricultural parastatals comprise mainly tea and sisal units; the mining parastatals comprise gems, diamonds, and salt units, the manufacturing parastatals relate to dairy, textiles, tobacco, coffee, cement, paper, shoes, bottling, printing, sugar, breweries, farm implements, bicycles, fibres, hides and skins, and engineering products; the public utilities comprise water and electricity; transport activity comprises roadways, railways, and pipeline; commercial activities, relate to trade, distribution and drugs, etc., and the others comprise banking, finance, insurance, real estates, buildings, wild life safaris, national tours, parks, lotteries, nutrition centres, and medical centres.

Thus, the government has stepped into all the key areas of the economy, and in the context of development, it would be necessary for the country to organise the deployment of its scarce resources in such a way that the objectives of the economy are realised within the framework of time and other constraints in question. In other words, the parastatals have done their best in maximising the production in the economy. But, during the last several years, there seems to be a general discontent and dissatisfaction that the parastatals have not come up to the public expectations; particularly when the economy is required to increase production, and overcome shortages and scarcities. The situation, therefore, necessitates an examination of the existing relationship of employment, wages and productivity, against the background indicated. It should however be pointed out that while productivity depends upon a number of factors such as the nature of the economy, the nature of the production function in use, the supply and demand for factors, the prices, the markets and the nature of competition, a general decline in productivity in the present context, may be broadly explained in terms of employment and wages in the economy of Tanzania.

Employment in the parastatals has increased more than five fold in the period 1976-77, from 19890 numbers to 105875, and the highest increase may be found in the manufacturing sector, which rose from 3619 to 43054. The other important activities, which have registered significant increases are agriculture, from 4736 to 16881, commerce from 3000 to 19286, and finance from 2049 to 9129. The following table gives picture of the diversification achieved by the economy in the decade in question in regard to the concentration or expansion or shifts in employment.

**Table 2.1** *Activity-wise Employment as per cent of Total Employment in Parastatals*

*(Percentages)*

| | *1966* | *1971* | *1977* |
|---|---|---|---|
| Agriculture | 23.81 | 28.58 | 15.94 |
| Mining | 14.05 | 31.55 | 26.05 |
| Manufacturing | 18.20 | 36.59 | 40.66 |
| Electricity | 9.10 | 3.42 | 3.56 |
| Construction | 25.52 | 4.64 | 2.92 |
| Commerce | 16.54 | 11.10 | 18.22 |
| Transport | 4.85 | 5.11 | 5.29 |
| Finance | 10.30 | 6.33 | 5.67 |

It may be observed that employment in the manufacturing sector has registered a substantial increase compared to the others, for the reason that the number of parastatals in this activity have risen by more than four times in the recent past, and that considerable expansion had also taken place in the capacity of the units. Also, as more firms have come under the administration of the parastatals, the ratio of employment under parastatals in relation to the government employment and the private sector employment has been growing steadily. This situation, as a whole serves one important purpose that, as the directly productive enterprises enter the organization of the parastatals, the enterprises belong to the state, and increasing profits in relation to capital invested in the firms, should lead to growth and further expansions in capacity. Such an examination made in respect of the increasing employment potential and the consequent wage bill, would give us an idea of the efficiency of the parastatals, if data are available. Such data are not available, and in the period under study, new firms have come into existence, which makes it difficult to bring to light efficiency indicators at micro and macro levels. The macro level data however, indicate the general nature of activity-wise profits as somewhat erratic, and in some cases losses persist.

We have so far traced the growing importance of the parastatals in the economy of Tanzania, the increase of numbers in the activities under consideration, and the nature of profits. Before we attempt an analysis of the productivity considerations, we deem it necessary to analyse the structure of wages, salaries and incentives and the real earnings in the parastatals for, the success of public enterprise depends, other things being equal, on the availability of skilled and efficient manpower for organising the various agricultural, industrial and other service-oriented enterprises. The wages and other related factors, particularly under conditions of inflation have an important role in the effective participation of the workers in the production processes.

In Tanzania, wage and salary earners represent only a small proporation of the total labour force, that is, those gainfully employed as well as those without recorded jobs. A large section of the labour force however includes self-employed persons, who fall under the private sector or the independent agricultural sector, and it is only in the recent years that the employment potential under the government and parastatals has been growing. The table given below shows that the share of the private sector in regular wage and salary employment has been on the decline. And within the public sector the parastatal sector has been gaining in its importance.

**Table 2.2:** *Wage and Salary Employment in Public and Private Sector*

*(Percentages)*

| | 1965 | 1966 | 1969 | 1970 | 1971 | 1972 | 1973 | 1974 |
|---|---|---|---|---|---|---|---|---|
| Private Enterprise | 62 | 60 | 39 | 38 | 37 | 37 | 32 | 30 |
| Public Sector | 38 | 40 | 61 | 62 | 63 | 63 | 68 | 70 |
| Parastatals | 28 | 26 | 41 | 42 | 44 | 44 | 51 | 47 |

**Source:** Survey of Employment and Savings 1965 - 1974.

The structure of employment in the parastatal sector shows that the given employment in this sector has been heavily dependent on the expansion of employment opportunities in the tertiary and service activities. Evidence indicates that for every one hundred persons, who were newly engaged in directly productive parastatal activities such as agriculture, mining, and manufacturing, between 1966 and 1969, there were 22 new entrants to the tertiary and service activities, and between 1970 and 1974, for every one hundred newly employed persons in directly productive parastatal activities, there were 260 new entrants into the tertiary and service sectors. Such an expansion in the tertiary sector seems to have been witnessed in the case of countries, which have experienced economic growth from low levels, and generally attributed to the growth of government functions and tertiary services more, that it is to industrialization itself. It is even pointed out that the public sector tends to employ a disproportionate number of the more highly skilled workers, and

**Table 2.3 :** *Wage Bill Paid : Public & Private Sectors 1963-1974*

*(mill. Shs.)*

| | 1965 | 1966 | 1969 | 1970 | 1971 | 1972 | 1973 | 1974 |
|---|---|---|---|---|---|---|---|---|
| Private Sector | 588 (55%) | 638 (54%) | 478 (35%) | 510 (32%) | 513 (32%) | 519 (31%) | 614 (29%) | 779. (24%) |
| Parastatal | 82 (15%) | 89 (15%) | 269 (23%) | 299 (28%) | 367 (30%) | 400 (30%) | 575 (40%) | 858 (40%) |

**Source:** Survey of Employment and earnings 1969-1974, Government of Tanzania.

this must also be true of the parastatals, considering their general expansion in activities. It is observed that the government and private wage employment account for almost nine tenths (87 per cent) of the workers who have had any university level education, with the reminder found among the self-employed, and that the concentration of young university college students in government is likely to persist for some years for the future.

Thus, in 1974-75, for each University graduate, who was newly employed outside the public sector, there were four graduates, who joined the public service, partly because of the tied up schemes of financing and partly because of the centralisation of the procedural process of allocation of high level manpower.

As regards the tremendous increase in the wage bill of the public sector (the parastatal wage bill alone increased six times) as a percentage of the total wage bill, it is attributed to the increase in the employment in the parastatal sector, and for the period 1969-74, the whole increment in the wage bill was brought about by increments in average wage rates. Thus, while the share of the public sector in the overall increment in the wage bill was 83 per cent during this period, 46 per cent of the increment in the public sector wage bill was accounted for by the increase in the average wage rate, whereas 31 per cent was due to a rise in employment. It is in this period that when the top salaries were frozen, and it is claimed that a good deal of the increase was due to increments in the earnings of employees at the bottom end of the wage scale in the public sector.

In a period of inflation, the increasing wage bill may not convey all that may be desired, for the impact of inflation in Tanzania, seems to have considerably eroded the worth of the minimum wage, and therefore, there seems to be a need for wage revisions keeping in mind the price indices, without which the overall efficiency may be hit adversely. It goes unsaid that, the workers and the fixed income groups, particularly the middle and the low income categories experience the effects of inflation more pointedly when prices of food items and essential commodities are on the increase.

In Tanzania, during the period 1960-76, the urban minimum wage has increased five times due to the revisions. Under the colonial rule, it was raised from 49 Shs. per month in 1960, to 107.50 Shs., an increase of 120 per cent. In 1961, it was increased from

107.50 Shs. to 130 per month, and two years later, it was revised to 150 Shs. in 1963, and to 170 in 1969. And, further increases to 240 Shs., 340 Shs. were made in 1972, 1974 and 1975 respectively. Thus, the minimum wage in 1975 was 124 per cent higher than in 1963, but these increases seem to hardly mean anything when we consider the question of inflation and the need for compensating for the rise in the cost of living index, as shown in the table below. The urban minimum wage has grown by a little more than twice, while the retail price index has increased by more than four times, and the real minimum wage had fallen by about sixty per cent with 1969 as the base year.

We may now consider the question of earnings of employees in the parastatals. The parastatals may be said to have assumed increasing importance in the late 1960s as a result of nationalisation and reorganisation of the enterprises. As regards the salaries of the personnel, the government appointed the SCOPO (the Presidential Standing Committee on Parastatal Organization) in 1967, for reviewing the salaries and benefits of employees so as to ensure that they are consistent with the salaries and allowances paid to employees in the public service requiring the skills and qualifications. Under the auspices of the SCOPO, fringe benefits in the parastatals have been scaled down to conform with those which exist in the civil service, although pay disparity between top salary earners in the two sectors still persist. And what is more important is not what the managers of the parastatals have not been getting, but what the others in similar positions with similar qualifications in the private sector have been getting in terms of salary and benefits. In this regard, it is mentioned that, Prof. Turner of the ILO recommended reductions in the pay at the top end of the salary structure in the private sector to match those which had been applied in the public sector, and that he warned that, any move to control top salaries in the public sector was deemed to failure if corresponding salaries in the private sector remained untouched. "There will, however, be anomalies in salaries between the public and private sectors, and a risk of losing able people from the public service unless this initiative is also followed in the private sector. The Employers' associations and business affiliates should be requested to advise their affiliates to revise their top salary scales in the line with the public initiative". (Turner Report I, Para 72, government of Tanzania, 1969).[2] This is also in line with one of the principles of Arusha Declaration that "the incomes of workers in the private sector are not very different from the incomes of workers in the public sector". (Government paper No. 4, Para 34). But there seems to be no real way of controlling the private sector salaries and benefits which are generally arranged in such a deft manner that they do not come under the scrutinty or purview or wrath of the government, and to the utter discomfort of the parastatal personnel. Thus, it may be pointed out that, effectively, the parastatal higher echelons of managerial personnel have suffered from the point of comparisons made between their own personnel in the lower wrungs of the ladder, and when compared with the contiguous positions in the civil service and in the private sector in matters of pay and perquisites. And while there are wide differences between the pay structure of parastatals and those of private firms, the hiatus tends to be greater with firms which are privately owned and controlled by foreigners who pay "well above SCOPO rates if a person is worth his job", and "each case is considered separately on merits and salary is based on experience, qualification, contribution to production and productivity", and where provisions exist for "periodical consideration to be existing salary levels and review" to obtain " higher standard candidates and given them incentives to improve productivity" and in this regard, the private foreign firms have their "own scales" for important positions. Thus, it may be said that the gap between public and private sectors' remuneration for upper occupations is quite significant and tends to increase with the seniority of the grade, and they "differ significantly for the last three highly - paid managerial staff, with private employers paying more than parastatal organisations". (Table 2.4).

It was pointed out at the Eighth Group Managers Conference of Zanzibar in 1978 that "Several parastatal organisations have lost good and skilled personnel simply because of the poor salaries they get". Private companies, which are not bound by the rigid rules of SCOPO have hired away qualified personnel out of the public owned organizations by offering them higher salaries and other fringe benefits". It is under such considerations that the salaries of highly skilled employees in general and artisans and plant managers in particular were marginally increased following the SCOPO Directive in 1979.

**Table 2.4 :** *Parastatals and Private Sector Salaries in Tanzania 1975*

(*Sh. per month*)

| *Category* | *Parastatals* | | *Private Sector* | |
|---|---|---|---|---|
| Skilled Workers | 476 | (1054) | 544 | (1088) |
| Lower Administrative Personnel | 510 | (986) | 612 | (1020) |
| Production Supervisory Personnel | 714 | (1700) | 816 | (1360) |
| Middle Management | 1224 | (1972) | (1530) | (5882) |
| Top management - local | 2316 | (3876) | 2856 | (3502) |
| Top management - non-local | 10370 | (13940) | (14430) | (23460) |

**Note :** Figures are average salaries based on the 1973 sample of 30 Tanzanian industries, figures in brackets indicate highest known salaries.

**Source :** Barker C.F., et al., eds, 1974/75, *Industrial Production and the Transfer of Technology in Tanzania. The Political Economy of Industrial Enterprises*, Dar-Es-Salaam, Institute of Development Studies, London.

In a recent study on inflation and wages in Tanzania, Valentine (1983) highlights the efforts of the government towards reducing income inequality between groups of wages and salary earners, particular in the light of inflationary circumstances and higher income tax rates, and the effect on production incentives, and points out that, the wage policy has "failed to influence positively productivity of labour by properly motivating workers". He emphasizes that the wage system (a) should function in such a way as to ensure an optimal distribution of national income among wages and salaries, profits, and government revenues, (b) aid in raising the productivity of labour, and (c) encourage reallocation of labour towards sectors of the economy and into activities in which demand is rising and where labour is most productive; and that, "wrong wage differentials will impede desirable transfers of labour, as well as the development of appropriate skills", and may even have "demoralising effect on the work force" in terms of general dissatisfaction and a possibility to convert the positions into sinecures. (Table 2.5)

It may be seen in the table that the average per worker monthly earnings increased by two times between 1966-77, while the general

**Table 2.5 :** *Parastatal Income, Wages, Productivity and Price Indices*

| | *Total Income of Parastatals (mill Shs.)* | *Total wages and salaries (Mill Shs.)* | *Total Number of workers* | *Average per workers Monthly earnings (Sh.)* | *Productivity Index (Sh.) (Sh.)* | *General Price Index 1969=100* | *Price Index for food items 1969= =100* |
|---|---|---|---|---|---|---|---|
| 1966 | 1159.6 | 88.7 | 19890 | 371.62 | 58300 | 93.0 | 98.2 |
| 1967 | 1803.1 | 162.5 | 26292 | 515.04 | 68579 | 95.4 | 99.9 |
| 1968 | 2225.8 | 237.6 | 36690 | 570.26 | 64162 | 198.0 | 101.3 |
| 1969 | 2457.9 | 282.6 | 49925 | 471.70 | 49231 | 100.0 | 99.7 |
| 1970 | 3200.8 | 340.2 | 54613 | 519.10 | 58608 | 103.7 | 103.3 |
| 1971 | 3706.1 | 391.3 | 67880 | 480.38 | 63543 | 107.4 | 108.5 |
| 1972 | 4682.9 | 466.3 | 68329 | 568.69 | 68534 | 118.6 | 120.1 |
| 1973 | 5869.4 | 555.1 | 71576 | 646.28 | 81826 | 129.3 | 135.1 |
| 1974 | 8373.1 | 714.9 | 80057 | 744.15 | 104589 | 169.0 | 177.2 |
| 1975 | 9557.2 | 781.8 | 82376 | 790.85 | 116019 | 248.5 | 265.8 |
| 1976 | 10457.2 | 949.4 | 92269 | 857.45 | 113317 | 306.7 | 323.0 |
| 1977 | 11488.3 | 950.3 | 105875 | 747.97 | 10808 | 358.4 | 386.3 |

**Source :** Computed from Analysis of Accounts of Parastatals 1966-1977.

price index and the price index for food articles has gone up by four times respectively, and the productivity of the parastatals as a whole, looked at from the total number of employees and the income earned by the parastatals has just risen by two times.

Thus, in the Tanzanian economy, the public enterprise activity has stepped into almost every aspect of economic life, leading to a general slow down of the economy, which may be partly attributed to lack of economic incentives and the prevalence of inflation. The government policy on the one hand, and inflation and income taxation on the other, have all brought a certain degree of equality in the "take-home" pay packets of all pay scales, and therefore, the question of application and acquisition of further skills and strengthening of human capital, an important means to furthering production and productivity seem to have experienced a set back. It is time the economy offers new incentives and at the same time control inflation. In the second instance, it would be necessary to examine the need for undertaking public activity indiscriminately without exploring possibilities of integration between enterprises, so as to achieve economies of scale, so that public activity steps into the most necessary and wider interiors of the economy. And before bringing about this integration, the government should identify those areas, which badly require public sector activity, and at the same time it should have the means and facility to function and operate more efficiently. Also, it is necessary to examine the need and practicability of a wage policy with appropriate functional disparities in the interest of instituting incentives. Finally, incorporation of real benefits to wage earners salary earners at levels may provide an impulse to the prosperity and well being of this community, for such real benefits existed in the past.

## REFERENCES

1. A parastatal enterprise is defined as a commercial organization owned by the Tanzanian government or with at least 50 per cent of the shares owned by the government.

2. The Report of H.A. Turner is the I.L.O. Report of 1967.

# 3

# Performance of the Manufacturing Parastatal Enterprises

The Government of Tanzania had shown a keen interest in expanding government activity and felt the need to evolve a policy towards public ownership, eversince it achieved independence in 1961. But the Three Year Development Plan (1961-64) and the First Five Year Development Plan (1964-69) could not do much on those lines until the Arusha Declaration (1967), which had explicitly committed Tanzania to a course of socialism and self reliance. The major means of production were subsequently to be owned and controlled by the workers and peasants. In the manufacturing sector, the major means of production were defined to include steel, machine tools, arms, automobiles, cement, fertilizer factories, textile industry, and all other major industry, which provides essential components for other industries. Outside the manufacturing sector, the major means of production covered banks, insurance companies, external and wholesale trade.

The philosophy behind the state intervention was that the economy should develop an indigenous entrepreneurship based on egalitarian principles of socialism and to reorient material production so as to ensure efficiency in factor use relative to domestic resource availability, thus fostering self reliance. In practice, however, the process of state intervention seems to have created a number of untoward and undesirable side effects. In particular, and particularly for the period 1978-83, there is a growing concern over the expanding state activity and in particular, over the performance of parastatal enterprises in Tanzania. From the point of the nation as such, there has been a need to overcome the persistently declining profitability of the parastatals which finally necessitate growing claims on the budget, and consequently lead to an inevitable resort to inflationary finance. From the point of view, of the development of the regions and establish the much needed linkages, the parastatals' inability to use economic resources efficiently has been a matter of grave concern to the planners. In terms of management and organisation, the state intervention has led to unfettered expantions in bureaucracy, uncoordinated and unproductive activities with utter lack of accountability.

The Three Year Development plan (1961-64) and the comprehensive First Five Year Plan (FFYP, 1964-69), emphasized the need to substitute domestic products for imports of consumer goods. Import substitution was seen as the ideal strategy for expanding and transforming the industrial sector. Both plans recognised the need to process local raw material for export, but while the Three Year Plan viewed this in terms of a long term possibility, the FFYP moved beyond this and incorporated in the agenda the processing of the key agricultural items, i.e., sisal and cashews for export. The FFYP also went beyond the Three Year Plan by introducing a wider range of import substitution activities, by including fertiliser, steel and oil refining, for the consideration of the planner for being produced locally. The main emphasis of the two plans was to achieve overall rapid economic growth, and to raise the share of manufacturing in total CDP by promoting the development of the industrial sector. These plans did not spell out the technical possibilities of the strategy inherent for such processes, nor did they pay any attention to such structural aspects as ownership, linkage effects, complementarity among industrial activities and across sectors, the question of comparative advantage, product mix, external economies and technology choice. Industrial development before 1967 was one of merely increasing the availability and accumulation of capital and very much within the inherited colonial pattern.

The government has taken several steps such as provision of guarantees for private foreign investment, and provision of facilities for repatriation of capital in the interest of encouraging investment opportunities and for reducing the crisis of capital shortage. The private sector was expected to generate about a third of total industrial investment during the FFYP, while the rest was to be financed by government investments which were generally externally financed. The market constraint was expected to ease as soon as the structure of the east African Common market was rationalised. The benefits of private international capital were thus expected to be taken advantage of by the African business community through technological transfer, capital availability and organization of skills, management, and marketing facilities.

**The Post Arusha Industrial Strategy**

The Arusha Declaration emphasized the need for intensification of state intervention as a pioneer of industrial activity in Tanzania. The Declaration has shown a strong preference for public ownership of all enterprises, and placed to commit a significant portion of new investments exclusively into the public sector. Reliance on foreign investment was to be cut down so as to be in line with the spirit of socialism and self-reliance. Immediately after the Declaration, state intervention took the form of nationalisation in full swing. At subsequent stages, state policy was directed towards acquisition of controlling (majority) shares among the existing private enterprises and the establishment of new publicly owned enterprises, so as to reduce the problem of financing the compensations which could have been of serious magnitudes.

A decade after Arusha Declaration, the number of manufacturing parastatals had grown from 17 to 43, after peaking to 47 in 1975. Besides the impact on ownership pattern and capital flows, the Declaration was also instrumental in initiating equity oriented policies. A new move was to introduce an incomes policy based upon an ILO report to minimise income disparities between urban workers and peasants. However, keeping in mind the questions of resource availability, priorities, and other problems of planning the backward economy, the economic policy was geared to initiate agricultural development so as to propitiate the atmosphere as well as surpluses for industrial development.

The Arusha Declaration, however, may be said to have recognized the importance of industrial development as part of the overall strategy. Import substitution was given a new blessing by the Second Five Year Plan (1969-74) which set the target rate of growth for manufacturing at 13 per cent, at a time when the rate of growth of GDP was around 6 per cent. President Nyerere declared that the country shall continue to expand simple manufacturing, the processing of primary commodities and the provision of basic construction materials, which was all that was possible in evolving the industrial strategy, and the better aspects of policy relate to widening of the base to include substitution of intermediate goods, initiation of manufacture for exports, decentralization of industry, and preference to labour intensive techniques. The question of what type of products should be produced, where-to sell and export, and the extent and direction of intersectoral linkages had remained unanswered.

## The Basic Industry Strategy

The Basic Industry Strategy enunciated at the end of the Second Plan was one of long term industrial strategy, articulated to remedy the inequalities of the Arusha Declaration. The overiding objective of the strategy is structural transformation and promotion of self-reliance, with suitable emphasis on the production of capital and high linkage goods. To facilitate self-reliance, emphasis was placed on the use of domestic raw materials, and production had to be strongly oriented towards the domestic market so as to meet the basic needs of the masses, by providing sectoral linkages. The strategy also outlined that agriculture had an important role to play as a generator of foreign exchange and as a supplier of raw materials. The basket of basic industries is defined broadly to incorporate wage goods (food and beverages, textile, leather and sisal), intermediate products (paper, wood and construction materials) and capital goods (iron and steel and chemicals).

### Performance of the Manufacturing Parastatal Sector

Substantial growth rates in real output between 1966-73 may be seen in rapid expansion of the manufacturing parastatal sector, while the 1974-75 economic crisis slowed down this momentum , which again picked up slightly during the coffee boom and the subsequent liberal import policy of 1976-77. An issue of immediate concern is the apparent fall in the growth of output particularly after 1978. Compare to the entire manufacturing sector, the parastatals appear to have fared worse; the rate of decline in growth has been on average higher in the parastatal sector than that of the entire manufacturing sector. As a result, the share of the value added, which had risen very sharply from 5.7 per cent in 1966 to a peak of 39.2 per cent in 1975 dropped to 18.5 per cent in 1982. As a percentage of total GDP, the parastatal value added in real terms fell from its 3.7 per cent peak in 1975 to 0.9 per cent in 1982 (Table 3.1). It would now be, therefore, interesting if we observe the trends in parastatal investment and employment.

**Investment**

The evolution of investment shares between 1966-80 may be seen in table 3.2. Absolute MP investment (fixed capital formation) shows two marked peak periods, i.e., 1970 and 1976 when it hits the Sh. 170 million mark twice. Otherwise, it has been fluctuating over time with a marked through between the two peak periods. However, the share of MP investment in total manufacturing investment rose sharply from a low base of 13.1 per cent in 1966 to a peak of 60.5 in 1970. Since then this share has been declining and by 1980 it was just 2 per cent higher its 1966 level (Table 3.2).

It is sometimes argued that, the slow down in parastatal output reflects the enlarged industrial base, while the vigorous growth, experienced between 1966-73 can be accounted for by the small industrial base. This argument seems to be incorrect because parastatal investment as a share of its value added was 26 per cent higher in 1970 than the 1966 level. With a higher proportion of investment to output in 1970, the growth rate should have been higher in the subsequent years. It is a matter of surprise, even the heavy flow of investment in 1970 and 1976 did not result in the expansion of output in the following years. Therefore, it is more likely that the slow down in the rate of industrial growth can not be explained fully by a fall in investment. While capacity creation took place, capacity utilization might have lagged behind installed capacity.

In this regard, an analysis of investmental capital output ratios may be necessary. Table 3.2 shows trends in the ICOR for the manufacturing Parastatal sector. It shows that the ICOR has been gradually rising from 1 in 1968 to 3.2 in 1972, with an ubrupt jump to 6.0 in 1975, reflecting stagnation of output during the crisis period. What is alarming is the negative characteristics of the 1977-80 period. This development generally indicates that for an extra shilling invested after 1976 it created less and less units of value added in the subsequent period. The ICOR may have to reflect a shift towards large social infrastructural investments which have long

**Table 3.1 :** *Value Added in Manufacturing 1966-1982*

*(1966 Prices)*

| Total | Manufacturing | | | *Parastatal manufacturing Manufacturing Enterprises* | | | |
|---|---|---|---|---|---|---|---|
| | MVA | Growth | MVA as % of Total GDP | Value added (Sd.) (mill.) | Rates of Growth % | Value Added as% of GDP | Value Added as% total MVA |
| 1966 | 525 | – | 8.1 | 30 | – | 0.5 | 5.7 |
| 1967 | 572 | 8.9 | 10.9 | 83 | 177.0 | 1.6 | 14.5 |
| 1968 | 611 | 6.8 | 11.0 | 109 | 31.3 | 1.9 | 17.8 |
| 1969 | 672 | 10.1 | 11.4 | 151 | 38.5 | 2.5 | 22.5 |
| 1970 | 716 | 6.5 | 9.3 | 195 | 29.1 | 2.5 | 27.2 |
| 1971 | 784 | 9.5 | 9.8 | 220 | 12.8 | 2.7 | 28.1 |
| 1972 | 850 | 8.4 | 10.0 | 264 | 20.0 | 3.1 | 31.0 |
| 1973 | 888 | 4.5 | 10.1 | 311 | 17.8 | 3.5 | 35.0 |
| 1974 | 900 | 1.3 | 10.0 | 333 | 7.0 | 3.7 | 37.0 |
| 1975 | 903 | 0.3 | 9.4 | 354 | 6.3 | 3.7 | 39.2 |
| 1976 | 961 | 6.4 | 9.5 | 358 | 11.3 | 3.5 | 37.2 |
| 1977 | 1017 | 3.3 | 9.4 | 393 | 9.8 | 3.6 | 38.6 |
| 1978 | 1051 | 2.0 | 9.2 | 348 | 3.0 | 3.0 | 33.1 |
| 1979 | 1029 | -2.0 | 8.5 | 304 | -13.0 | 2.5 | 29.5 |
| 1980 | 893 | -13.0 | 7.1 | 299 | -30.0 | 2.4 | 33.5 |
| 1981 | 761 | -15.0 | 6.4 | 206 | -31.0 | 1.7 | 27.1 |
| 1982 | 568 | -25.4 | 4.9 | 105 | -51.0 | 0.9 | 18.5 |

**Source :** (1) National Accounts of Tanzania 1966-1980
(2) Analysis of Accounts of Parastatals 1966-1977
(3) Haliya Uchumi wa Taifa Katika Mwaka, 1982.

gestation lags, a shift towards more capital intensive investments, and a growing deterioration in the efficiency use of capital and other related productive inputs, or a combination of these developments. As far as the parastatals are concerned, the first development may have to ruled out, and the large infrastructural investments such as the TAZARA Project, the TANZAM Highway and the TAZAMA Pipeline that dominated government investment in the 1970s fell outside this sector. There is also evidence to suggest that a combination of (ii) and (iii) might have occured, though.

**Table 3.2** : *Manufacturing Investment Shares 1966-1980*

(*At 1966 prices*)

| | *Manuf. Investment as % of total Monetary Sector Investment* | *MP Investment (Shs. million)* | *MP investment as% of total Manufacturing Investment* | *MP Investment as % of MP Value added.* |
|---|---|---|---|---|
| 1966 | 14.0 | 20 | 13.1 | 67 |
| 1967 | 16.8 | 62 | 35.6 | 75 |
| 1968 | 17.9 | 40 | 19.4 | 38 |
| 1969 | 14.8 | 50 | 33.1 | 33 |
| 1970 | 17.0 | 170 | 60.5 | 93 |
| 1971 | 13.3 | 145 | 54.5 | 66 |
| 1972 | 11.8 | 91 | 49.4 | 34 |
| 1973 | 12.6 | 101 | 49.5 | 32 |
| 1974 | 14.9 | 94 | 33.8 | 28 |
| 1975 | 17.3 | 93 | 32.7 | 26 |
| 1976 | 27.2 | 170 | 32.7 | 47 |
| 1977 | 41.5 | 160 | 19.8 | 41 |
| 1978 | 36.8 | 145 | 18.5 | 42 |
| 1979 | 36.3 | 161 | 16.6 | 53 |
| 1980 | 34.0 | 118 | 15.1 | 39 |

**Source :** (1) National Accounts of Tanzania 1966-80
(2) Analysis of Accounts of Parastatals, 1966-77
(3) Haliya Uchumi Katika Mwaka, 1983.

Table 3.2 gives an estimate of capital intensity and capital productivity, using depreciation as a proxy measure of capital.

A favourable decrease in capital intensity is seen with the declining capital labour (K/L) ratio during the period 1967 to 1970, and after 1972 the K/L ratio has continued to rise up to 1978 indicating a gradual shift towards capital intensive production processes. Since capital utilisation relates to the way fixed capital is used jointly with other inputs, particularly labour, rising capital intensity may imply higher labour productivity, and hence a corresponding higher rate of growth of output, the evidence suggests that this did not happen, though.

**Table 3.3 :** *ICOR, Capital Output and Capital Labour Ratio in Manufacturing*

| | *Total Manufacturing ICOR* | *Manufacturing ICOR* | *Manufacturing K/O Ratio* | *Parastatal K/L Ratio* |
|---|---|---|---|---|
| 1968 | 3.5 | 1.0 | 1.98 | 24,567 |
| 1969 | 3.7 | 1.5 | 1.92 | 23,482 |
| 1970 | 3.7 | 2.1 | 1.64 | 20,707 |
| 1971 | 3.9 | 3.3 | 1.82 | 16,369 |
| 1972 | 4.3 | 3.2 | 2.04 | 18,200 |
| 1973 | 5.6 | 2.9 | 2.44 | 25,680 |
| 1974 | 12.5 | 3.2 | 2.76 | 26,453 |
| 1975 | 10.7 | 6.0 | 2.88 | 28,913 |
| 1976 | 9.3 | 5.6 | 2.79 | 26,012 |
| 1977 | 10.9 | −70.5 | 2.93 | 26,710 |
| 1978 | 30.9 | −31.6 | 3.40 | 27,100 |
| 1979 | −20.6 | −5.0 | 4.20 | 23,797 |
| 1980 | — | — | 4.50 | 25,987 |

**Source :** *National Accounts of Tanzania 1966-1980* : Analysis of Parastatal Accounts 1966-1977 Haliya Uchumi Wa Taifa Katika Mwaka, 1982, also see MSD Bagachwa and S. Chandrasekhar, "Performance of the Manufacturing Parastatal Enterprises in Tanzania", in *The Role of Public Sector in the Economic Development of Tanzania*, International Seminar, ARUSHA, 1984.

It is already noted that the rate growth of output has been declining since 1973 although capital intensity has been rising since then. Secondly, the parastatal value added per person in real terms declined from Shs. 15,654 in 1967 to Shs. 12,227 in 1969, and picked up slightly in 1970 and stagnated between 1972-76. During the 1967-81 period, real output per person in the sector has never recovered the 1967 level, and in fact a discernible declining trend is seen between 1976 and 1981. More seriously, real output per worker in 1981 was 4 times lower than that of 1967.

And except for 1967, on an average, productivity per worker in the sector was less than that of the entire manufacturing sector in each of the subsequent years implying that the average annual labour productivity in the private manufacturing sector might have been higher than that of the parastatal in the respective years.

**Employment**

In spite of the fact that output per person has been declining, the parastatals have managed to expand opportunities of industrial employment. The average annual growth of real output has been declining more quickly than that of employment particularly for the period 1976-81, and the parastatal absòlute employment rose by 15 times between 1966-79 compared to that of the entire sector, which increased 3 times. Whereas employment generation in one of the objectives of Tanzania's industrial policy, one has to be sure that an additional job created is at least as productive as the previous job. Thus, with the growth of labour productivity lagging behind, the seemingly successful parastatal employment may.be said to be more obvious than real.

And the deterioration in the effectiveness of capital input is further reinforced by a gradual but consistent rise in the capital output (K/O) ratio for the period 1970-81, indicating that capital productivity (value added per unit of capital) in real terms has been declining over the period under consideration. With both labour and capital productivity declining, it may be argued that overall or total factor productivity in the parastatal might have fallen.

**Capacity Utilization**

The deterioration of capital productivity in the manufacturing parastatals may also be due to excess capacity. Underutilization of capacity not only raises the capital intensity (*i.e.*, K/L ratio) of the firm, but also results in lower output per unit of capital invested, and the problem of idle industrial capacity has been a widespread phenomenon of the developing economies. In Tanzania, particularly, the capacity utilization rates have on average continued to fall below their historic levels, as may be seen from Table —3.5, which helps us the 1981 production with that of the previous years. It may be observed that except for cement, aluminium and fertilizer products, the 1981 production capacity was below peak production of the previous period for the rest 15 industries. The second measure is more revealing as it considers both installed and actual capacity in a given year. It is also apparent that except for cigarettes, rolled steel and batteries, the 1980 capacity utilization levels were below the 1976 levels for the rest 7 of the selected industries.

**Table 3.4 :** *Trends in Manufacturing Employment 1966-1981*

| | *Manufacturing Employment* | | *Manufacturing Parastatal Employment* | | |
|---|---|---|---|---|---|
| | *Number* | *Growth Rate %* | *Number* | *Growth Rate* | *as % of total manufacturing Employment* |
| 1966 | 30,276 | – | 3,619 | – | 12.0 |
| 1967 | 34,157 | 1.13 | 5,302 | 46.5 | 15.5 |
| 1968 | 42,387 | 24.0 | 8,792 | 65.9 | 20.7 |
| 1969 | 43,767 | 3.3 | 12,350 | 40.5 | 28.2 |
| 1970 | 48,699 | 11.3 | 15,454 | 25.1 | 31.7 |
| 1971 | 50,869 | 4.5 | 24,836 | 60.7 | 48.8 |
| 1972 | 55,114 | 8.3 | 25,387 | 2.2 | 46.0 |
| 1973 | 63,355 | 15.0 | 29,595 | 16.6 | 46.7 |
| 1974 | 69,974 | 10.4 | 34,778 | 17.5 | 49.7 |
| 1975 | 73,218 | 4.6 | 35,278 | 1.4 | 48.2 |
| 1976 | 75,005 | 2.4 | 38,443 | 8.9 | 51.3 |
| 1977 | 78,090 | 4.0 | 43,054 | 12.0 | 55.1 |
| 1978 | 97,111 | 24.0 | 43,541 | 24.9 | 55.4 |
| 1979 | 107,577 | 10.8 | 53,788 | 4.0 | 48.3 |
| 1980 | 103,896 | −4.0 | 51,948 | −4.0 | 49.0 |
| 1981* | 102,842 | −1.0 | 50,420 | −3.0 | 50.0 |

**Sources :** (1) Economic Surveys (various years); and
(2) Haliya Uchumi Katika Mwaka 1982.

Supply constraints have generally been identified as the principal cause of underutilization of capacity in Tanzanian industry. The phenomenon of increasing capital intensity, the absence of a developed capital goods sector, and the measures introduced by the Bank of Tanzania tighten imports in the interest of balancing the trade operations, resulted in insufficient supplies of imported inputs and spare parts, generally, and the problem becomes even more difficult in the face of inadequate maintenance and managerial and development services. Also, the fluctuations in agricultural output due to drought or flood reduces the supply of raw materials to industries. The other serious trade cap is posed by the energy crises and shortage of water supply needed by the various types of industry.

**Table 3.5 :** *Rates of Capacity Utilization for Selected Industries*

| | *1981 as % of (Peak Year) production* | | *Capacity Utilization 1976 %* | *Capacity Utilization 1980 %* |
|---|---|---|---|---|
| Textiles | 97.6 | (1975) | 92 | 47 |
| Beer | 74.9 | (1978) | 84 | 75 |
| Cigarettes | 81.6 | (1980) | 77 | 86 |
| Cement | 100.00 | (1981) | 72 | 51 |
| Petroleum | 68.3 | (1972) | 99 | 78 |
| Iron Sheets | 33 | (1978) | 50 | — |
| Enamel ware | 6.5 | (1971) | — | — |
| Blankets | 32.1 | (1973) | 14 | 12 |
| Fishnets | 23.3 | (1977) | — | — |
| Aluminium | 100.00 | (1981) | — | — |
| Sisal Ropes | 42.0 | (1979) | — | — |
| Pyrethrum extract | 19.1 | (1972) | — | — |
| Wheat Flour | 29.7 | (1978) | — | — |
| Canned Meat | 16.3 | (1974) | — | — |
| Batteries | 97.5 | (1980) | 60 | 83 |
| Shoes | 66.2 | (1976) | 62 | 30 |
| Rolled Steel | 88.7 | (1979) | 35 | 61 |
| Fertilizer | 100.00 | (1981) | 40 | 38 |

**Source :** Bank of Tanzania, Economic and Operations Reports 1966, 1982. Column 2 and 3 are from Skarstein, 1983.

The performance of manufacturing parastatals judged in terms of the surplus generated has been somewhat encouraging up to 1977. Absolute gross surplus in real terms rose from Shs. 18.2 million in 1966 to Shs. 244 million in 1977. For the period between 1966-73 the real surplus grew at the same pace with the growth of real value added, but after 1977 however, real surplus has been declining faster than real value added, which is reflected in the falling rate return on capital for the period 1977-80. The decline in gross surplus may be explained by a combination of the following interelated factors : falling output declining labour productivity, excess capacity and a sharp rise in the wages and other costs of production.

Samuel Wangwe examined the problem of allocation of resources in the industrial sector in Tanzania during the balance of payments crisis since the mid-1970s. It is argued that the slow growth of industrial output in the 1970s was aggravated by the failure to shift the utilization of foreign exchange away from capital goods inputs for capacity expansion in favour of intermediate inputs for capacity utilization. Consequently the economy benefited only moderately from considerable new investments in the decade due to

**Table 3.6 :** *Manufacturing Parastatal Surplus, Rate of Return and Wages*

| | *Gross Absolute (Sh. mill)* | *Surplus rates of growth* | *Real capital stock (Sh. mill)* | *Real Rate of Return %* | *Nominal Wages (Sh. mill)* | *Real Wages + (Sh. mill)* |
|---|---|---|---|---|---|---|
| 1966 | 18.2 | – | 34 | 53.0 | 11.8 | 11.8 |
| 1967 | 48.0 | 163.0 | 138 | 35.0 | 36.7 | 35.0 |
| 1968 | 46.0 | −5.0 | 216 | 21.3 | 50.9 | 43.0 |
| 1969 | 91.0 | 98.0 | 290 | 31.4 | 71.2 | 60.0 |
| 1970 | 92.5 | 1.1 | 320 | 29.0 | 94.3 | 90.5 |
| 1971 | 110.0 | 20.0 | 400 | 27.5 | 119.0 | 110.0 |
| 1972 | 136.8 | 24.3 | 540 | 25.3 | 150.1 | 127.2 |
| 1973 | 166.6 | 21.8 | 760 | 21.8 | 186.3 | 144.4 |
| 1974 | 149.6 | −10.0 | 920 | 16.3 | 282.4 | 183.4 |
| 1975 | 191.0 | 28.0 | 1020 | 18.7 | 318.7 | 163.0 |
| 1976 | 206.0 | 7.9 | 1000 | 20.6 | 320.1 | 152.0 |
| 1977 | 244.0 | 18.4 | 1150 | 21.2 | 342.6 | 149.0 |
| 1978 | 230.0 | −5.0 | 1180 | 19.5 | 362.0 | 118.0 |
| 1979 | 176.0 | −24.0 | 1280 | 13.7 | 491.0 | 139.0 |
| 1980 | 164.0 | −7.0 | 1350 | 12.1 | 604.0 | 171.0 |

**Source :** (1) Analysis of Accounts for Parastatals 1966-77.
(2) Haliya Uchumi wa Taifa Katika Mwaka 1982.

reduced efficiency in the use of resources. The aspect of misallocation of resources was explained in terms of the role of foreign finance on the one hand and the weak link between macro-level and micro-level planning on the other.[1]

The value added in the manufacturing sector registered a declining trend since about 1972-73, and precipitated by the oil crisis and drought of 1973-74, leading to a diversion of foreign exchange resources, until the coffee boom of the period 1976-77 and 1977-78 restored the health of the economy partially and temporarily, for the boom did not last long. The end of the decade had witnessed a deeper foreign exchange crisis triggered by a second round of oil price increase, high interest rates, and weakened commodity markets coincided with drought and border conflicts with Uganda, resulting in a further deceleration of the annual value added growth to –2.1 per cent in 1979, –13.2 per cent in 1980 and –28.2 per cent in 1981, and its share in GDP declined from 10 per cent in 1974 to 7.1 per cent in 1980 and down to 5.8 per cent in 1981.

And, during the period 1966-80, while the manufacturing value added doubled, industrial employment had tripled. During the 1970-80 period, the share of manufacturing employment in total wage employment increased from 12.9 per cent in 1970 to 15.9 per cent in 1978, and to 16 per cent in 1980, which is explained in terms of the continued rate of investment at a high rate through the 1970s due to the establishment of several new enterprises, and the older enterprises expanded even if they had to operate at lower capacities, and with a negative marginal contribution to industrial output. The result of these developments was considerable underutilization of labour in manufacturing especially in the past 1978 period.

The manufacturing investments, however, increased five to six times between 1966 and 1980, much faster than the total investment in the economy, *i.e.*, from 12 to 15 per cent in early 1970s to about 36 per cent at the end of the decade, suggesting an increasing capital output ratio and capital labour ratio, suggesting an indication of inefficient use of capital in that large investments were associated with less than large increments in output, specifically in textiles, cement and shoes. Supported by a sample of industries, Wangwe, argues that since the rate 1970s especially, the inefficient use of capital was quite obvious in a number of industries in which capacity expansions were made. Also considerable investments were also made in new industrial activities such as bicycles, insulated wire and cables, billet casting, pharmaceuticals, which were not out of several organizational and technological predicaments.

In addition, over the decade, imports of capital goods increased faster than imports of intermediate goods, the former three-fold in value terms, while the latter doubled, and the failure to shift the balance of imports away from capital goods is said to have pronounced the low capacity utilization rates in the period. In 1979, when the balance of payments crisis was pervading, the value of capital goods imports increased by 28.8 per cent over the previous year, compared to only 12.6 per cent in the intermediate goods.

It is also argued that there is no evidence of an explicit policy to curtail imports of capital goods and encourage imports of intermediate goods due to the fact that it has been easier for importers to obtain suppliers' credit for longer periods as preferred by the government for capital goods, rather than for intermediate goods imports, which had generated a built in bias towards the danger. The potential magnitude of the bias is indicated by the share of foreign finance in the total invisible funds which was of the order of 60 per cent, suggesting the need for a twist in policy for shifting the incidence of foreign aid in favour of more critical demands for intermediate goods so as to strengthen the existing capacities.[2]

**Problems of Organization of Parastatals**

The organization of parastatals consists of a number of levels, such as the (*a*) Economic Committee of Cabinet which has the ultimate authority, and reviews and approves long term sectoral development plans and all management agreement contracts, (*b*) the Ministries of Finance and Economic Planning which control the selection and financing of parastatal projects, (*c*) the Ministry of Industries which has direct control on the Holding Corporations and their subsidiaries, having equity shares and also provide various specialized services for this subsidiaries or parastatals, and (*d*) the Board of Directors of the respective companies which has the power for major decisions.

In addition, the manufacturing parastatals face a number of other controls from the Bank of Tanzania (BOT) which is the licensing authority for capital imports, the National Bank of Commerce (NBC) controls, which is the major source of working capital loans, the Treasury which has the right to check the use of profits and the distribution of dividents, the Prices Commission which sets and controls products prices. Also, Management agreements have to be approved by the Economic Committee of the Cabinet, and the SCOPO sets and regulates wage rates. The permanent labour Tribal (PLT) has the authority to approve all labour agreements. The Ministry of Trade administers tariff rebates and in conjunction with the Bank of Tanzania approves industrial export permits. These major regulatory agencies apart, the directives of the Headquarters of the multinational corporations, and the influe-

**Table 3.7 :** *Trends in Value Added in Manufacturing 1961-1980 at 1966 Prices*

| *Year* | *Value Added in Mfg (T. Shs. Mill)* | *Annual Change (%)* | *Share in GDD (%)* |
|---|---|---|---|
| 1961 | 283 | | 3.6 |
| 1962 | 313 | + 10.8 | 3.7 |
| 1963 | 317 | +1.3 | 3.4 |
| 1964 | 394 | +24.4 | 7.1 |
| 1965 | 446 | +13.2 | 7.7 |
| 1966 | 525 | +17.7 | 8.1 |
| 1967 | 572 | +9.0 | 8.4 |
| 1968 | 611 | +6.8 | 8.6 |
| 1969 | 672 | +10.0 | 9.3 |
| 1970 | 716 | +6.5 | 9.3 |
| 1971 | 784 | +9.5 | 9.8 |
| 1972 | 850 | +8.4 | 10.0 |
| 1973 | 888 | +4.5 | 10.1 |
| 1974 | 900 | +1.4 | 10.0 |
| 1975 | 903 | +0.3 | 9.5 |
| 1976 | 961 | +6.4 | 9.5 |
| 1977 | 1017 | +5.8 | 9.4 |
| 1978 | 1051 | +3.3 | 9.2 |
| 1979 | 1029 | —2.1 | 8.5 |
| 1980 | 893 | —13.2 | 7.1 |
| 1981 | 648 | —28.2 | 5.8 |

**Source :** Samuel Wangwe, "Industrialization and Resource Allocation in a Developing Country : The Case of Recent Experiences in Tanzania," *World Development*, Vol. 11, No. 6, pp. 483-492, 1983.

nces of the political party executives, place the prospects of the growth of industry in a state of perpetual jeopardy.

**Table 3.8 :** *Employment in Manufacturing 1963-1980*

| *Year* | *Number of Employees in Mfg* | *Annual Change (%)* | *Share of Manufacturing Employment in Total Wage Employment (%)* |
|---|---|---|---|
| 1963 | 22,212 | | 6.5 |
| 1964 | 23,583 | 6.2 | 6.7 |
| 1965 | 25,729 | 9.1 | 7.7 |
| 1966 | 29,390 | 14.2 | 8.7 |
| 1967 | 34,157 | 16.2 | 9.9 |
| 1968 | 42,387 | 24.1 | 11.7 |
| 1969 | 43,396 | 2.4 | 11.8 |
| 1970 | 48,314 | 11.3 | 12.9 |
| 1971 | 53,516 | 10.8 | 13.6 |
| 1972 | 62,118 | 16.1 | 15.3 |
| 1973 | 63,355 | 2.0 | 13.4 |
| 1974 | 69,974 | 10.4 | 14.5 |
| 1975 | 73,218 | 4.6 | 15.6 |
| 1976 | 75,003 | 2.4 | 15.7 |
| 1977 | 78,090 | 4.1 | 15.7 |
| 1978 | 81,216 | 4.0 | 15.9 |
| 1979 | 85,493 | 3.5 | 15.6 |
| 1980 | 89,255 | 4.4 | 16.0 |

**Source :** *World Development*, Vol. 11, No. 6, pp. 483-492, 1983.

**Table 3.9 :** *Investment in Manufacturing, 1966-1980*

| *Year* | *Investment in Mfg. (T. Shs. Million 1966 Prices)* | *Annual Change (%)* | *Share of Industrial Investment in Total Investment (%)* |
|---|---|---|---|
| 1966 | 153 | | 15.6 |
| 1967 | 174 | +13.7 | 14.8 |
| 1968 | 206 | +18.3 | 16.2 |
| 1969 | 151 | —26.7 | 13.2 |
| 1970 | 281 | +86.1 | 17.0 |
| 1971 | 266 | —5.3 | 13.4 |
| 1972 | 185 | —30.5 | 11.0 |
| 1973 | 204 | +10.3 | 11.8 |
| 1974 | 277 | +35.8 | 15.6 |
| 1975 | 294 | +6.1 | 17.9 |
| 1976 | 520 | +76.9 | 26.6 |
| 1977 | 719 | +38.2 | 37.2 |
| 1978 | 779 | +8.3 | 36.7 |
| 1979 | 962 | +23.5 | 36.9 |
| 1980 | 781 | —18.8 | 33.8 |

**Source :** *World Development*, Vol. 11, No. 6, pp. 483-492, 1983.

**Table 3.10 :** *Capital Goods and Intermediate Goods Imports, 1971-1980*

(*Current prices*)

| *Year* | *Machinery and Transport Equipment (T. Shs. Million)* | *Annual Change (%)* | *Intermediate Inputs Except Petroleum (T. Shs. Million)* | *Annual Change (%)* |
|---|---|---|---|---|
| 1971 | 996 | | 803 | |
| 1972 | 894 | −10.2 | 839 | +4.5 |
| 1973 | 1023 | +14.4 | 1060 | +26.3 |
| 1974 | 1304 | +27.5 | 1442 | +36.0 |
| 1975 | 1653 | +26.8 | 1279 | −11.3 |
| 1976 | 1789 | +8.2 | 1274 | —0.4 |
| 1977 | 2297 | +28.4 | 1388 | +8.9 |
| 1978 | 3564 | +55.2 | 1850 | +33.3 |
| 1979 | 4589 | +28.8 | 2084 | +12.6 |
| 1980 | 3529 | −23.1 | 1614 | −21.3 |
| 1971-1979 | | +18.5 | | +11.2 |
| 1971-1980 | | +13.5 | | +7.4 |

**Source :** *World Development*, Vol. 11, No. 6, pp. 483-492, 1983.

**Table 3.11 :** *Capacity Creation and Capacity Utilization in Selected Manufacturing Industries, 1976-1980*

| *Industry* | *Units* | *Qc 1976* | *Qc 1980* | *Δ Qc 1976-1980* | *Qa 1976* | *Qa 1980* | *Δ Qa 1976-1980* |
|---|---|---|---|---|---|---|---|
| 1. Textiles | sq m (mill.) | 90 | 200 | 110 | 75 | 93.5 | +18.5 |
| 2. Cement | '000 tons | 340.0 | 1100 | 760 | 244.5 | 326.0 | +81.5 |
| 3. Beer | bill. cases | 6.3 | 6.8 | 0.5 | 5.3 | 5.1 | –0.2 |
| 4. Cigarettes | mill. pcs | 4.8 | 5.5 | 0.7 | 3.7 | 4.9 | +1.2 |
| 5. Paints | '000 1. | 5035.4 | 5631.2 | 595.8 | 3159 | 1376 | –1783 |
| 6. Fertilizers | '000 tons | 105 | 134 | 29.0 | 41.6 | 54.4 | +12.8 |
| 7. Shoes | mill. pairs | 6 | 14 | 8.0 | 4 | 5.3 | +1.3 |
| 8. Tyres and tubes | '000 pcs | 438 | 538 | 100 | 375 | 432.3 | +57.3 |
| 9. Leather | mill. sq ft | 11.8 | 32.5 | 20.7 | 7.8 | 16.5 | +8.7 |
| 10. Hoes/ploughs | '000 tons | 1.2 | 3.0 | 1.8 | 1.69 | 1.94 | +0.25 |
| 11. Corrugated iron sheets | '000 tons | 52 | | | 30.0 | 21.4 | –8.6 |
| 12. Blankets | mill. pcs | 6 | 6 | 0 | 0.86 | 0.73 | –0.13 |
| 13. Dry cells | mill. pcs | 96 | 96 | 0 | 54.8 | 76.7 | +21.9 |
| 14. Steel | '000 tons | 30 | 30 (36) | 0(6) | 12.2 | 18.9 | +6.7 |
| 15. Bags | mill. pcs | 10 | 10 (17) | 0(7) | 3.7 | 5.3 | +1.6 |
| 16. Sugar | '000 tons | 115 | 195 | 80 | 110.0 | 119.3 | +9.3 |

**Source :** *World Development*, Vol. 11, No. 6, pp. 483-492, 1983.

The problem with these controls is that they are not coordinated, and the objectives of the organizations are widely different. The parastatal may be frustrated by the prices set by the Prices Commission, and may be grilled by the foreign exchange rules of the Bank of Tanzania in crucial situations. The Holding Corporations according to the Report of the World Bank (1975), have Financial and Operations departments whose functions duplicate those of their subsidiaries. The problem is further aggravated by the recent proliferation and multiplicity of Holding Manufacturing Corporations. Coordination, therefore, is generally difficult and the bureaucracy takes cover under the available rules for lapses in accountability and failures of the Organization.

## REFERENCES

1. Sammel Wangwe in M. Samkichaka and Chandrasekhar, op. cit.

2. Sammel wangwe in *World Development*, op. cit.

# 4

# Conclusion

Political independence to the economy of Tanzania seems to have conferred a colossal crisis in terms of its inability to take adequate steps to transform the traditional economy into the modern ones. An important obstacle in this regard seems to be its incapacity to devise a realistic format of political philosophy consistent with the need to the hour. There is also a certain lack of administrative efficiency to gear up the body politic for implementing the various social and economic schemes of the government, and for the containment of rising prices, rising deficits and increasing shortages, so as to pave the way for a reasonable rate of growth. During the last two decades, therefore, the compounding problems of the economy have manifested in a rampant inflation, deficits on account of current revenue, deficits on account of foreign trade, a decline in agricultural production, and an inadequate performance of industry, in spite of the additions made to industrial capacities and capital stock at a cost which have economy cannot absorb easily.

That the objective of equity sadly conflicts the objective of growth may be seen in practice in the Tanzanian experience. At a time when the economy was poised to achieve stability and growth, the country achieved independence, and therefore set the socialist scheme of things on an acceptably sound precept and perception, but not in terms of the system that the economy deserves. In fact the system could not be made viable with the resources available, and what was perceived as a system was not consistent with expectations. The economy could not have achieved the expected growth given the deployment of available resources in terms of self-reliance and freedom. The socialist yearning divested the economy of considerable foreign assistance and expertise in economic management, and the available meagre resources were least adequate for the various deserving channels. At the same time, there prevails an atmosphere of uncertainty and helplessness fraught with economic shortages, ever increasing prices, growing taxes, increasing administrative controls with rising government activity, falling agricultural and industrial production, and the rising debt burden, consequent to the inevitable dependence on aid and support and expensive imports, which only brings into relief, the contradiction involved in the path adopted to progress. A greater contradiction relates to the unproductive expansion of bureaucracy and the stretching of government into several enterprises least conducive to economy, which resulted in public expenditures of sorts. The need of hour is to control sickness and hunger, produce the most essential commodities, provide incentives to increase agricultural production, provide amenities, and social inputs such as roads and communications, hospitals and housing, and ameliorate poverty levels, under the auspices of public and private enterprise and foreign assistance, and promote a value free economy until stability is restored.

It has been an accepted phenomenon that most governments in modern times have shown the tendency to devote a large part of their current revenue to the finance of expenditures of a capital nature. And there are fewer governments, at the same time, which have not shown segacity and shrewdness to explore fresh avenues of taxation, while increasing intermittently or incessantly, the rates and burden of existing taxes, as might suit them. And without exception, all the governments in the developed and the developing societies have shown a helpless aptitude for extensive reliance on indirect taxation. This seems to be happening in spite of the fact that most such taxes tend to become regressive, particularly in the poorer societies. And the taxes of the type of excises seem to be relied upon the greater, in spite of the fact of their cascading effects and the proven shifting which takes place, the burden of which the ultimate consumer bears, and the general effects of the system manifest in terms of additions to existing inflation. The economy of Tanzania seems to be no exception to the general rule.

Another interesting aspect of this economy is that government seems to have taken upon itself a number of operations through the parastatals in addition to the normal activities. But there seems to be no evidence of the policies being implemented successfully. In each and every activity that the government has entered, there exists a powerful private sector which is unbridled by regulations and control, and an even more powerful informal sector which is practically unaccounted under the existing monetary and financial system. It is these activities which generate the unaccounted money and the much needed resilience for most people to live with inflation.

An important consequence of the Arusha Declaration of the policy of socialism and self-reliance was, the nationalisation of all the expatriate financial entities and the commercial banks, and the establishment of the other specialised financial institutions engaged in financing industry, commerce, trade, agriculture, insurance business, and the mobilization of savings for investment. This was essential because, before nationalisation, the accumulated funds in the banking institutions were a subject of capital flights, and were utilized elsewhere. But unfortunately, the banking system did not seem to have risen to the expectations of policy, for the reason that the financial institutions have degenerated into inefficient monopolistic firms reinforced with bureaucratic checks and controls leading to unproductive operations. In addition, they lack the necessary financial capital for their operations, and the activity of mobilization of savings may be said to have been totally neglected.

Thus, the major ailments affecting the economy have been in terms of falling growth rates, rising prices, increasing imports in relation to exports, inadequate resource mobilisation of funds, inadequate, infrastructure, inability to finance social and economic development programmes and the general failure to initiate progress built on economic incentives in all sectors of the economy. Under such circumstances, it would be in the fitness of things to look at the problems more openly and with greater sense of realism than proceed ideologically. This requires the economy to reduce checks and controls in public life, reduce bureaucratic restrictions, confine public activity to the most desired areas so as to reduce the cost of administration which may also reduce the burden of taxation in the economy, as a whole. The situation also calls for greater and more liberal participation of international partners in the development processes of the economy, and what may be true of the Tanzanian economy may also generally hold good to such other African economies.

# Bibliography


1. Bagachwa, MSD. "The Dar-es-Salaam Urban Informal Sector Survey", in ILO/JASPA, *Basic Needs in Danger*, Addis Abbaba, ILO, 1982.

2. Bagachwa, MSD. "A Survey of Small Scale Enterprises in Tanzania", in M. Sambichaka and S. Chandrasekhar, *Economic Research Bureau*, 1984.

3. Bank of Tanzania *Bank of Tanzania, Its Role and Functions*, Dar-se-Salaam, 1979.

4. Bienefeld, M.A. "Evaluating Industrial Performance between 1961 and 1978" in M. Fransman (Ed.), *Industry and Accumulation in Africa*, London, Heinemann, 1982.

5. Bienefeld, M.A. *Tanzanian Industry and Basic Needs : Short and Long Term Issues*, Dar-se-Salaam, 1981.

6. Bruce A. Bloomstrom. "Capital Flight in East Africa, the Case of Uganda", in Tom J. Farer, (Ed.), *Financing African Development*, Cambridge, Mass : MIT, 1965.

7. Clark, W.E. *Socialist Development and Public Investment in Tanzania*, University of Toronto Press, 1978.

8. Due F. John and Jean M. Due. "The Financing of the Southern Region and Other Regional Governments of the Sudan", *International Bureau of Fiscal Documentation*, 1982.

9. Due F. John. "A Comparison of Four Manufacturers Sales Taxes - Ghana, Kenya, Tanzania, Zambia, Barbados, Iceland", *Bulletin*, Vol. XXX, November 11, 1976.

10. Due F. John and Jean M. Due. "The Challenges faced by Four African Economies, Zimbabwe, Zambia, Tanzania and the Sudan", Faculty *Working Paper* No. 958, University of Illinois, May 1983.

11. Frank Ellis. "Agricultural Pricing Policy in Tanzania 1970-79, Implications for Agricultural Output : Rural Incomes and Crop Marketing Costs", *ERB Paper 80.3*, University of Dar-es-Salaam.

12. Gershenberg, Irving. "Multinationals and Development : Commercial Banking in Uganda", *African Today*, No. 4, 1974.

13. Green, Rwegasira and Van Arkadie. *Economic Stocks and National Policy-Marking, Tanzania in the 1970s*, The Hague : Institute of Social Studies, 1980.

14. Gulhati, R. and Uday Sekhar. "Industrial Strategy of late Starters : The experience of Kenya, Tanzania and Zambia", *World Development*, Vol. 10, No. 11, Nov. 1982.

15. Hyuha, Mukwanason. An Econometric Analysis of Financial Intermediation, Saving and Investment in Uganda", University of Dar-es-Salaam, *Economic Research Bureau*, 1981.

16. Hyuha, Mukwanason "Financial Intermediaries and Economic Growth in Developing Countries", *Journal of Economic Reflections*, Vol. II, No. 1, 1982.

17. Hyuha, Mukwanason. "Financial Structure and Economic Development in Africa : Some Evidence" University of Dar-es-Salaam, *Economic Research Bureau*, 1983.

18. International Bank for Reconstruction and Development. *The Economic Development of Tanganyika*, The John Hopkins Press, 1961.

19. International Labour Organization. *Towards Self Reliance : Development, Employment and Equity Issues in Tanzania*, Addis Abbaba : 1978.

20. ILO-JASPA. *Basic Needs of Danger* : *A Basic Needs Oriented Development Strategy for Tanzania*, Addis Abbaba : 1982.

21. Kaduma and Modi. *Tax Reform Planning in the United Republic of Tanzania*, Ministry of Finance, 1969.

22. Munanka, EMB. "Industrial Integration, Diversification and Performance : Case of Tanzania", in LA Msambichaka and S. Chandrasekhar, *Economic Research Bureau*, 1984.

23. ILO-JASPA. *Towards Self Reliance Development Employment and Equity Issues in Tanzania*, 1978.

24. Msambichaka, L.A. and S. Chandrasekhar. *Readings of Economic Policy of Tanzania*, Economic Research Bureau, University of Dar-es-Salaam, 1984.****

25. Msambichaka, L.A. "Agricultural Development in Tanzania, Problems and Priorities", in LA Msambichaka and S. Chandrasekhar, *Economic Research Bureau*, 1984.

26. Mukwanason Hyuha "Financial Intermediaries and the Saving-Investment Process in Uganda", *A Ph. D. thesis*, University of Alberta, Canada, 1980.

27. "The Financial Superstructure in Tanzania, Prospects and Problems", in L.A. Msambichaka and S. Chandrasekhar, *Economic Research Bureau*, 1980.

28. Ndulu, B.J. "Investment Patterns and Impacts in the Post Arusha Tanzania", in L.A. Msambichaka and S. Chandrasekhar, Readings of Economic Policy of Tanzania, *Economic Research Bureau*, 1984.

29. Nyerere, J.K. "Public Ownership in Tanzania" in TANU, *The Arusha Declaration*, 1967.

30. Nyerere, J.K. "Uzamaa—The Basis of African Socialism", in *Freedom and Unity*.

31. Nyerere Julius K. "The Arusha Declaration" in *Ugamaa Essays on Socialism*, Oxford University Press, New York, 1968.

32. *Freedom and Socialism,* Oxford University Press, 1968.

33. *Freedom and University*, Oxford University Press, 1966.

34. Nyirabu Charles M. *Banking Policies and Priorities in Tanzania in the 1980s*, Dar-es-Salaam, Bank of Tanzania, 1980.

35. Phillips, David. "Industrialization in Tanzania Small Scale Production, Decentralization, and Multi-technology Programme for Industrial Development", *Economic Research Bureau*, University of Dar-es-Salaam, 1976.

36. Rweikiza Baguma. "Agricultural Development Policies and Problems of Implementation", in L.A. Msambichaka and S. Chandrasekhar, *Economic Research Bureau*, 1984.

37. Rweyamamu, S. *Underdevelopment and Industrialization in Tanzania*, Oxford, University Press, Nairobi, 1973.

38. Sayeeda Bano. "Tanzania's Balance of Payments", in L.A.

Msambichaka and S. Chandrasekhar, *Economic Research Bureau*, 1984.

39. TANU. *The Arusha Declaration and TANU's Policy on Socialism and Self-Reliance*, Dar-es- Salaam, 1967.
40. Tibaijuka A.K. and Msambichaka, L.A. "The Role of Large Scale Farming in Tanzania, in L.A. Msambichaka and S. Chandrasekhar, *Economic Research Bureau*, 1984.
41. UNIDO. *Country Industrial Development Study of the United Republic of Tanzania, Draft Report*, TISCO Project Report No. 80-71, Dar-es-Salaam, 1981.
42. UNIDO *The Potential for Resource - Based Industrial Development in the LDCs*, No. 3, United Republic of Tanzania, February, 1982.
43. United Republic of Tanzania. "Wages, Incomes, Rural Development, Investment and Price Policy", *Government Paper No. 4*, Dar-es-Salaam, Government Printer, 1967.
44. World Bank. *Basic Economic Report on Tanzania*, Annex 5, Industry, (Washington DC 1977).
45. Wangwe, S.M. "Factors Influencing Capacity Utilization in Tanzanian Manufacturing", *International Labour Review*, Vol. 115, No. 1, Jan/Feb, 1977.
46. World Bank. *Capital Utilization in Developing Countries*, 1981.
47. Wagao, H. Jumane. *Income Distribution in a Developing Economy, The Case of Tanzania*, University of Sussex, 1981.
48. Wangwe, S.M. and M. Collanie "Structure and Development of the Engineering Sector in Tanzania", *Economic Research Bureau Paper 77.11,* University of Dar-es-Salaam, 1977.
49. Wangwe, S.M. "Capacity Utilization and Capacity Creation in Manufacturing in Tanzania with Special reference to the Engineering Sector", *Ph. D. thesis*, University of Dar-es-Salaam, 1979.
50. Wangwe, S.M. "The Industrial Development Experience : Some Structural Imbalances", in L.A. Msambichaka and S. Chandrasekhar, *Economic Research Bureau*, 1984.
51. Wangwe, Samuel M. "Industrialization and Resource Allocation in a Developing Country : The Case of Recent Experiences in Tanzania", *World Development*, Vol. 11, No. 6, pp. 483-492, 1983.

# INDEX